100 BIBLE PROMISES FOR

DIFFICULT TIMES

SMITH FREEMAN
Publishing

Contents

100 BIBLE PROMISES FOR DIFFICULT TIMES

A Message to Readers

*We know that all things work together for the good of those
who love God: those who are called according to His purpose.*
ROMANS 8:28 HCSB

God's Word promises that all things work together for the good of those who love Him. Yet sometimes we encounter situations that seem so troubling that we simply cannot comprehend how those events might be a part of God's plan for our lives. We experience tough times, and we honestly wonder if recovery is possible. But with God, all things are possible.

The Christian faith, as communicated through the words of the Holy Bible, is a healing faith. It offers comfort in times of trouble and hope instead of hopelessness. Through the healing words of God's promises, we are taught that the Lord continues to manifest His plan in good times and bad.

This book contains 100 Bible promises that every Christian should trust *and* live by. The ideas in these chapters are intended to serve as powerful reminders—reminders of God's commandments, reminders of God's promises, reminders of God's gifts, and reminders of God's love.

Adversity is not meant to be feared, it is meant to be worked through. If this text assists you, even in a small way, as you move through and beyond your own tough times, it will have served its purpose. May God bless you and keep you today, tomorrow, and forever.

1

THE PROMISE: GOD'S GIFT OF ETERNAL LIFE IS AVAILABLE TO YOU

I assure you: Anyone who hears My word and believes
Him who sent Me has eternal life and will not come
under judgment but has passed from death to life.
JOHN 5:24 HCSB

God has promised that you can receive a priceless gift—a gift beyond compare, a gift of infinite value. That gift is, of course, the gift of eternal life. That gift, freely given by God's only begotten Son, is the priceless possession of everyone who accepts Christ as Lord and Savior.

Thankfully, God's grace is not an earthly reward for righteous behavior; it is a truly priceless spiritual gift that can be accepted by believers who commit their lives to God's only begotten Son.

The promise of eternal life is the ultimate gift, and it allows us to maintain perspective during difficult times because we know that our earthly hardships are temporary, but heaven is eternal. So we should praise the Lord for His blessings; we should share His Good News with all who cross our paths; and we should keep our problems in perspective. We return our Father's love by accepting His grace and by sharing His message in good times *and* difficult times. When we do, we will be blessed now and forever.

MORE THOUGHTS ABOUT ETERNAL LIFE

Death is not the end of life;
it is only the gateway to eternity.
BILLY GRAHAM

Death is not a journey into an unknown land;
it is a voyage home. We are going, not to
a strange country, but to our Father's house.
JOHN RUSKIN

Everything that is joined to the immortal Head
will share His immortality.
C. S. LEWIS

You need to think more about eternity and not less.
RICK WARREN

At most, you will live a hundred years on earth,
but you will spend forever in eternity.
RICK WARREN

More from God's Word

*For God so loved the world, that he gave his
only begotten Son, that whosoever believeth in him
should not perish, but have everlasting life.*
JOHN 3:16 KJV

*For the wages of sin is death, but the gift of God
is eternal life in Christ Jesus our Lord.*
ROMANS 6:23 NIV

*I have written these things to you who believe
in the name of the Son of God, so that you
may know that you have eternal life.*
1 JOHN 5:13 HCSB

*The world and its desires pass away,
but whoever does the will of God lives forever.*
1 JOHN 2:17 NIV

The last enemy that will be destroyed is death.
1 CORINTHIANS 15:26 NKJV

Remember This

If you have already welcomed Christ into your heart as your personal
Savior, then your future is secure. If you're still sitting on the fence,
the time to accept Him is this very moment.

2

THE PROMISE: WHEN TIMES ARE TOUGH, HE CAN HEAL YOUR HEART

He heals the brokenhearted and binds up their wounds.
PSALM 147:3 HCSB

All of us encounter occasional disappointments and setbacks. These occasional visits from Old Man Trouble are inevitable, and none of us are exempt. When tough times arrive, we may be forced to rearrange our plans and our priorities, but even on our darkest days, we must remember that God's love remains constant. And we must never forget that the Lord intends for us to use our setbacks as stepping stones on the path to a better life.

The fact that we encounter adversity is not nearly as important as the way we choose to deal with it. When tough times arrive, we have a clear choice: we can begin the difficult work of tackling our troubles, or not. When we summon the courage to look Old Man Trouble squarely in the eye, he usually blinks. But if we refuse to address our problems, even the smallest annoyances have a way of growing into king-sized catastrophes.

Psalm 145 promises, "The LORD is near to all who call on him, to all who call on him in truth. He fulfills the desires of those who fear him; he hears their cry and saves them" (v. 18–20 NIV). And the words of Jesus offer us comfort: "These things I have spoken to you, that in Me you may have peace. In the world you will have tribulation; but be of good cheer, I have overcome the world" (John 16:33 NKJV).

As believers, we know that God loves us and that He will protect us. In times of hardship, He will comfort us; in times of sorrow, He will dry our tears. When we are troubled or weak or sorrowful, the Lord is always with us. We must build our lives on the rock that cannot be shaken: we must trust in God. And then we must begin tackling our problems because if we don't, who will? Or should?

More Thoughts about Tough Times

*Often the trials we mourn are really gateways
into the good things we long for.*
Hannah Whitall Smith

*God will not permit any troubles to come upon
us unless He has a specific plan by which
great blessing can come out of the difficulty.*
Peter Marshall

*Jesus does not say, "There is no storm."
He says, I am here, do not toss, but trust."*
Vance Havner

*As we wait on God, He helps us use
the winds of adversity to soar above our problems.
As the Bible says, "Those who wait on the LORD . . .
shall mount up with wings like eagles."*

BILLY GRAHAM

*If God sends us on stony paths,
He provides strong shoes.*

CORRIE TEN BOOM

MORE FROM GOD'S WORD

*We are hard-pressed on every side,
yet not crushed; we are perplexed,
but not in despair.*

2 CORINTHIANS 4:8 NKJV

*I called to the LORD in my distress;
I called to my God.
From His temple He heard my voice.*

2 SAMUEL 22:7 HCSB

*The LORD is my rock, my fortress, and my deliverer,
my God, my mountain where I seek refuge.
My shield, the horn of my salvation,
my stronghold, my refuge, and my Savior.*

2 SAMUEL 22:2–3 HCSB

*God blesses those who patiently endure testing
and temptation. Afterward they will receive the crown
of life that God has promised to those who love him.*

The LORD is my shepherd; I shall not want.
PSALM 23:1 KJV

A TIMELY TIP

If you're having tough times, don't hit the panic button and don't keep everything bottled up inside. Talk things over with people you can really trust. A second opinion (or, for that matter, a third, fourth, or fifth opinion) is usually helpful. So if your troubles seem overwhelming, be willing to seek outside help. Your family members, friends, and mentors can help you regain perspective and build a better future. So don't hesitate to ask for their advice, their help, and their prayers.

3

THE PROMISE: IF YOU HAVE FAITH, YOU CAN MOVE MOUNTAINS

For truly I say to you, if you have faith the size of a mustard seed, you will say to this mountain, "Move from here to there," and it will move; and nothing will be impossible to you.

MATTHEW 17:20 NASB

Because we live in a demanding world, all of us have mountains to climb and mountains to move. Moving those mountains requires faith. And the experience of trying, with God's help, to move those mountains inevitably builds character.

Every life—including yours—is a series of wins and losses. Every step of the way, through every triumph and tragedy, God walks with you, ready and willing to strengthen you and protect you. So the next time you're being tested, remember to take your fears to God. If you call upon Him, you will be comforted. Whatever your challenge, whatever your trouble, God can help you handle it. And He will help you handle it *if* you ask Him.

When you place your faith, your trust, indeed your life in the hands of your heavenly Father, you'll be blessed during good times and hard times. So strengthen your faith through praise, through worship, through Bible study, and through prayer. And trust God's plans. With Him, all things are possible, and He stands ready to open a world of possibilities to you *if* you have faith.

More Thoughts about Faith

*Faith is confidence in the promises of God
or confidence that God will do what He has promised.*
CHARLES STANLEY

*I do not want merely to possess a faith;
I want a faith that possesses me.*
CHARLES KINGSLEY

*Shout the shout of faith. Nothing can withstand
the triumphant faith that links itself to omnipotence.
The secret of all successful living lies in this shout of faith.*
HANNAH WHITALL SMITH

*Faith does not concern itself
with the entire journey. One step is enough.*
LETTIE COWMAN

*How do you walk in faith? By claiming the promises
of God and obeying the Word of God, in spite of
what you see, how you feel, or what may happen.*
WARREN WIERSBE

More from God's Word

Don't be afraid, because I am your God.
I will make you strong and will help you;
I will support you with my right hand that saves you.
Isaiah 41:10 NCV

Don't be afraid. Only believe.
Mark 5:36 HCSB

Blessed are they that have not seen,
and yet have believed.
John 20:29 KJV

All things are possible for the one who believes.
Mark 9:23 NCV

And he said unto her, Daughter,
thy faith hath made thee whole;
go in peace, and be whole.
Mark 5:34 KJV

A Timely Tip

Today, think about the times you've been hesitant to share your faith. And as you contemplate the day ahead, think about three specific ways that you can strengthen your faith by sharing it with family and friends.

4

THE PROMISE: THE LORD CAN GIVE YOU THE COURAGE AND THE STRENGTH TO MEET ANY CHALLENGE

Be strong and courageous, and do the work. Do not be afraid or discouraged, for the LORD God, my God, is with you.
1 CHRONICLES 28:20 NIV

When times are tough, fears have a way of dominating our thoughts and hijacking our emotions. No wonder we are tempted to search for short-term solutions to long-term problems.

When you're experiencing difficult times, you will inevitably be faced with a series of decisions, and it takes courage to make the right ones. You may be faced with a choice between doing the right thing or the easy thing. If so, you must summon the courage to follow your conscience. And while you're summoning that courage, you should ask God for His help.

Billy Graham observed, "Down through the centuries, in times of trouble and trial, God has brought courage to the hearts of those who love Him. The Bible is filled with assurances of God's help and comfort in every kind of trouble which might cause fears to arise in the human heart. You can look ahead with promise, hope, and joy." Dr. Graham's words apply to you.

The next time you find your courage tested by difficult circumstances, remember that God is as near as your next breath. He is your shield and your strength; He is your protector and your deliverer. Call upon Him in your hour of need and then be comforted. Whatever your challenge, whatever your trouble, God can help you rise above it. No exceptions.

More Thoughts about Courage

Take courage. We walk in the wilderness today and in the Promised Land tomorrow.
D. L. Moody

Courage is not simply one of the virtues, but the form of every virtue at the testing point.
C. S. Lewis

Just as courage is faith in good, so discouragement is faith in evil, and, while courage opens the door to good, discouragement opens it to evil.
Hannah Whitall Smith

In my experience, God rarely makes our fear disappear. Instead, He asks us to be strong and take courage.
Bruce Wilkinson

*Do not let Satan deceive you into being
afraid of God's plans for your life.*
R. A. TORREY

MORE FROM GOD'S WORD

*Be on guard. Stand firm in the faith.
Be courageous. Be strong.*
1 CORINTHIANS 16:13 NLT

*For God has not given us a spirit of fearfulness,
but one of power, love, and sound judgment.*
2 TIMOTHY 1:7 HCSB

I can do all things through Him who strengthens me.
PHILIPPIANS 4:13 NASB

But He said to them, "It is I; do not be afraid."
JOHN 6:20 NKJV

*Behold, God is my salvation;
I will trust, and not be afraid.*
ISAIAH 12:2 KJV

A TIMELY TIP

Is your courage being tested today? Cling tightly to God's promises,
and pray. God can give you the strength to meet any challenge, and
that's exactly what you should ask Him to do.

5

THE PROMISE: WHEN YOU PUT GOD FIRST, HE WILL PROVIDE FOR YOUR NEEDS

But seek first the kingdom of God and His righteousness,
and all these things will be provided for you.
MATTHEW 6:33 HCSB

When difficult times arrive, as they do from time to time, pressures begin to mount. We have long lists of obligations at home, at work, and many places in between. From the moment we rise until we drift off to sleep at night, we have things to do and things to think about. So how do we find time for God? We must *make* time for Him, plain and simple.

When we put God first, we're blessed. But when we succumb to the pressures and distractions of everyday life, we inevitably pay a price for our misguided priorities. In the book of Exodus, God warns that we should put no gods before Him. Yet all too often, we place our Lord in second, third, or fourth place as we focus on other things. When we yield to the countless distractions that surround us, we forfeit the peace that might otherwise be ours.

In the wilderness, Satan offered Jesus earthly power and unimaginable riches, but Jesus refused. Instead, He chose to worship His heavenly Father. We must do likewise by putting God first and worshiping Him only. God must come first. Always first.

More Thoughts about Putting God First

We become whatever we are committed to.
RICK WARREN

*Worship in the truest sense takes place
only when our full attention is on God—
His glory, majesty, love, and compassion.*
BILLY GRAHAM

One with God is a majority.
BILLY GRAHAM

*When all else is gone, God is still left.
Nothing changes Him.*
HANNAH WHITALL SMITH

*To God be the glory, great things He has done;
So loved He the world that He gave us His Son.*
FANNY CROSBY

More from God's Word

You shall have no other gods before Me.
EXODUS 20:3 NKJV

Therefore, whether you eat or drink,
or whatever you do, do all to the glory of God.
1 CORINTHIANS 10:31 NKJV

For this is the love of God, that we keep His commandments.
And His commandments are not burdensome.
1 JOHN 5:3 NKJV

How happy is everyone who fears the LORD,
who walks in His ways!
PSALM 128:1 HCSB

But prove yourselves doers of the word,
and not merely hearers who delude themselves.
JAMES 1:22 NASB

A Timely Tip

Think about your priorities. Are you *really* putting God first in your life, or are you putting other things—things like material possessions or personal status—ahead of your relationship with the Father. And if your priorities for life seem somewhat misaligned, think of at least three things you can do today to put God where He belongs: in first place.

6

THE PROMISE: THE LORD IS ALWAYS FAITHFUL

Let us hold on to the confession of our hope without wavering,
for He who promised is faithful.
HEBREWS 10:23 HCSB

The Bible contains promises upon which you, as a believer, can depend. When the Creator of the universe makes a pledge to you, He will keep it. In fact, you can think of the Bible as a written contract between you and your heavenly Father. When you fulfill your obligations to Him, the Lord will most certainly fulfill His covenant to you.

When we accept Christ into our hearts, God promises us the opportunity to experience contentment, peace, and spiritual abundance. But more importantly, God promises that the priceless gift of eternal life will be ours. These promises should give us comfort. With God on our side, we have absolutely nothing to fear in this world and everything to hope for in the next.

Are you tired? Discouraged? Fearful? Be comforted and trust the promises that God has made to you. Are you worried or anxious? Be confident in God's power. Do you see a difficult future ahead? Be courageous and call upon the Lord. He will protect you and then use you according to His purposes. Are you confused? Listen to the quiet voice of your heavenly Father. He is not a God of confusion. Talk with Him; listen to Him; trust Him, and trust His promises. He is steadfast, and He is your Protector forever.

More Thoughts about God's Promises

There are four words I wish we would never forget, and they are, "God keeps His word."
Charles Swindoll

The stars may fall, but God's promises will stand and be fulfilled.
J. I. Packer

We honor God by asking for great things when they are a part of His promise. We dishonor Him and cheat ourselves when we ask for molehills where He has promised mountains.
Vance Havner

The promises of Scripture are not mere pious hopes or sanctified guesses. They are more than sentimental words to be printed on decorated cards for Sunday school children. They are eternal verities. They are true. There is no perhaps about them.
Peter Marshall

Gather the riches of God's promises. Nobody can take away from you those texts from the Bible which you have learned by heart.
Corrie ten Boom

More from God's Word

Sustain me as You promised, and I will live;
do not let me be ashamed of my hope.
Psalm 119:116 HCSB

As for God, his way is perfect: the word of the Lord is tried:
he is a buckler to all those that trust in him.
Psalm 18:30 KJV

They will bind themselves to the Lord with an
eternal covenant that will never again be forgotten.
Jeremiah 50:5 NLT

My God is my rock, in whom I take refuge,
my shield and the horn of my salvation.
2 Samuel 22:3 NIV

He heeded their prayer, because they put their trust in him.
1 Chronicles 5:20 NKJV

A Timely Tip

Today, think about the role that God's Word plays in your life. And while you're at it, remind yourself of the promises He has made to you. When you do, you will worry less and trust Him more.

7

The Promise: You Need Not Remain Focused on Your Past

Do not remember the former things, nor consider the things of old. Behold, I will do a new thing.

ISAIAH 43:18–19 NKJV

The American theologian Reinhold Niebuhr composed a profoundly simple verse that came to be known as the Serenity Prayer: "God, grant me the serenity to accept the things I cannot change, the courage to change the things I can, and the wisdom to know the difference." Niebuhr's words are far easier to recite than they are to live by. Why? Because most of us want life to unfold in accordance with our own wishes and timetables. But sometimes God has other plans.

One of the things that fits nicely into the category of "things we cannot change" is the past. Yet even though we know that the past is unchangeable, many of us continue to invest energy worrying about the unfairness of yesterday when we should, instead, be focusing on the opportunities of today and the promises of tomorrow.

Author Hannah Whitall Smith observed, "How changed our lives would be if we could only fly through the days on wings of surrender and trust!" These words remind us that even when we cannot understand the past, we must trust God and accept His will.

So if you've endured a difficult past, accept it and learn from it, but don't spend too much time here in the precious present fretting over memories of the unchangeable past. Instead, trust God's plan and look to the future. After all, the future is where everything that's going to happen to you from this moment on is going to take place.

More Thoughts about Accepting the Past and Moving on with Life

Don't waste energy regretting the way things are or thinking about what might have been. Start at the present moment—accepting things exactly as they are—and search for My way in the midst of those circumstances.
Sarah Young

Our past experiences may have made us the way we are, but we don't have to stay that way.
Joyce Meyer

Trust the past to God's mercy, the present to God's love and the future to God's providence.
St. Augustine

Don't be bound by the past and its failures. But don't forget its lessons either.
Billy Graham

More from God's Word

One thing I do, forgetting those things which
are behind and reaching forward to those things
which are ahead, I press toward the goal for
the prize of the upward call of God in Christ Jesus.
PHILIPPIANS 3:13–14 NKJV

Have mercy on me, O God, according to your unfailing love;
according to your great compassion blot out my transgressions.
Wash away all my iniquity and cleanse me from my sin.
PSALM 51:1–2 NIV

Your old sinful self has died,
and your new life is kept with Christ in God.
COLOSSIANS 3:3 NCV

He restoreth my soul: he leadeth me
in the paths of righteousness for his name's sake.
PSALM 23:3 KJV

And He who sits on the throne said,
"Behold, I am making all things new."
REVELATION 21:5 NASB

A Timely Tip

The past is past, so don't live there. If you're focused on the past, change your focus. If you're living in the past, it's time to stop living there, starting now.

8

THE PROMISE: YOU CAN PRAY CONFIDENTLY

*The earnest prayer of a righteous person has great power
and produces wonderful results.*

JAMES 5:16 NLT

God promises that your prayers are powerful; so pray. Pray about matters great and small; and be watchful for the answers that God most assuredly sends your way.

Is prayer an integral part of your daily life or is it a hit-or-miss routine? Do you "pray without ceasing," or is your prayer life an afterthought? Do you regularly pray in solitude, or do you bow your head only when others are watching?

The quality of your spiritual life will be in direct proportion to the quality of your prayer life. Prayer changes things, and it changes you. Today, instead of turning things over in your mind, turn them over to the Lord in prayer. Instead of worrying about your next decision, ask God for answers. Don't limit your prayers to meals or to bedtime. Pray constantly and confidently. God is listening; He wants to hear from you; and you most certainly need to hear from Him.

MORE THOUGHTS ABOUT PRAYER

*Prayer is not a work that can be allocated
to one or another group in the church. It is everybody's
responsibility; it is everybody's privilege.*

A. W. TOZER

Prayer connects us with God's limitless potential.

HENRY BLACKABY

*God shapes the world by prayer. The more praying
there is in the world, the better the world will be,
and the mightier will be the forces against evil.*

E. M. BOUNDS

*Prayer shouldn't be casual or sporadic,
dictated only by the needs of the moment. Prayer should
be as much a part of our lives as breathing.*

BILLY GRAHAM

*God wants to remind us that nothing on earth
or in hell can ultimately stand against the man
or the woman who calls on the name of the Lord!*

JIM CYMBALA

More from God's Word

Rejoice always, pray without ceasing, in everything give thanks;
for this is the will of God in Christ Jesus for you.
1 Thessalonians 5:16–18 NKJV

Anyone who is having troubles should pray.
James 5:13 NCV

I desire therefore that the men pray everywhere,
lifting up holy hands, without wrath and doubting.
1 Timothy 2:8 NKJV

Don't worry about anything, but in everything,
through prayer and petition with thanksgiving,
let your requests be made known to God.
Philippians 4:6 HCSB

The Lord is far from the wicked,
but he hears the prayer of the righteous.
Proverbs 15:29 NIV

A Timely Tip

Prayer is always necessary, but it's absolutely essential during difficult times. Martin Luther observed, "If I should neglect prayer but a single day, I should lose a great deal of the fire of faith." Those words apply to you, too. And it's up to you to live—and to pray—accordingly.

9

THE PROMISE: WHEN YOU TRUST THE LORD, HE WILL DIRECT YOUR PATH

*Trust in the LORD with all your heart, and lean not
on your own understanding; in all your ways
acknowledge Him, and He shall direct your paths.*

PROVERBS 3:5–6 NKJV

The Bible promises that when you trust the Lord, He will guide your steps and light your path. Thankfully, whenever you're willing to talk with God, He's willing to listen. And the instant that you decide to place Him squarely in the center of your life, He will respond to that decision with blessings that are too unexpected to predict and too numerous to count.

On occasion, you will confront circumstances that trouble you to the very core of your soul. It is during these difficult days that you must find the wisdom and the courage to trust your heavenly Father despite your circumstances.

The next time you find your courage tested to the limit, lean upon God's promises. Trust His Son. Remember that God is always near and that He is your protector and your deliverer. When you are worried, anxious, or afraid, call upon Him. God can handle your troubles infinitely better than you can, so turn them over to Him. Remember that God rules both mountaintops and valleys with limitless wisdom and love—now and forever.

MORE THOUGHTS ABOUT TRUSTING GOD

*One of the marks of spiritual maturity is
the quiet confidence that God is in control,
without the need to understand why He does what He does.*
CHARLES SWINDOLL

*Faith and obedience are bound up
in the same bundle. He that obeys God,
trusts God; and he that trusts God, obeys God.*
C. H. SPURGEON

*When a train goes through a tunnel and it gets dark,
you don't throw away your ticket and jump off.
You sit still and trust the engineer.*
CORRIE TEN BOOM

Never be afraid to trust an unknown future to a known God.
CORRIE TEN BOOM

*Never yield to gloomy anticipation. Place your hope
and confidence in God. He has no record of failure.*
LETTIE COWMAN

More from God's Word

In quietness and trust is your strength.
ISAIAH 30:15 NASB

The LORD is my rock, my fortress, and my deliverer,
my God, my mountain where I seek refuge.
My shield, the horn of my salvation,
my stronghold, my refuge, and my Savior.
2 SAMUEL 22:2–3 HCSB

The fear of man is a snare, but the one
who trusts in the LORD is protected.
PROVERBS 29:25 HCSB

Those who trust in the LORD are like Mount Zion.
It cannot be shaken; it remains forever.
PSALM 125:1 HCSB

Jesus said, "Don't let your hearts be troubled.
Trust in God, and trust in me."
JOHN 14:1 NCV

Remember This

Because God is trustworthy—and because He has made promises to you that He intends to keep—you are protected. The Lord always keeps His promises. Trust Him.

10

THE PROMISE: BECAUSE GOD IS FAITHFUL, YOU CAN ALWAYS HAVE HOPE

Let us hold fast the confession of our hope without wavering,
for He who promised is faithful.
HEBREWS 10:23 NASB

There are few sadder sights on earth than the sight of a man or woman who has lost all hope. In difficult times, hope can be elusive, but those who place their faith in God's promises need not worry. After all, God is good; His love endures; He has offered each of us the gift of eternal life.

Yet despite God's promises, despite Christ's love, and despite our countless blessings, we are frail human beings who can still become discouraged from time to time. When we do, we need the encouragement of Christian friends, the life-changing power of prayer, and the healing truth of God's holy Word.

If you find yourself falling into the spiritual traps of worry and discouragement, seek the healing touch of Jesus and the encouraging words of fellow believers. And if you find a friend in need, remind him or her of the peace that is found through a personal relationship with Jesus. It was Christ who promised, "These things I have spoken unto you, that in me ye might have peace. In the world ye shall have tribulation: but be of good cheer; I have overcome the world" (John 16:33 KJV).

This world can be a place of trials and tribulations, but as believers, we are secure. God has promised us peace, joy, and eternal life. And, of course, the Creator keeps His promises today, tomorrow, and forever.

More Thoughts about Hope

Faith looks back and draws courage;
hope looks ahead and keeps desire alive.
John Eldredge

If your hopes are being disappointed just now,
it means that they are being purified.
Oswald Chambers

The presence of hope in the invincible
sovereignty of God drives out fear.
John Piper

Down through the centuries in times of trouble and trial, God
has brought courage to the hearts of those who love Him. The
Bible is filled with assurances of God's help and comfort
in every kind of trouble which might cause fears to arise in the
human heart. You can look ahead with promise, hope, and joy.
Billy Graham

More from God's Word

This hope we have as an anchor of the soul,
a hope both sure and steadfast.
HEBREWS 6:19 NASB

I say to myself, "The LORD is mine,
so I hope in him."
LAMENTATIONS 3:24 NCV

The LORD is good to those who wait for Him,
to the soul who seeks Him. It is good
that one should hope and wait quietly
for the salvation of the LORD.
LAMENTATIONS 3:25-26 NKJV

Hope deferred makes the heart sick.
PROVERBS 13:12 NKJV

Be strong and courageous,
all you who put your hope in the Lord.
PSALM 31:24 HCSB

A Timely Tip

If you're experiencing hard times, you'll be wise to start spending more time with God. If you do your part, the Lord will do His part. So never be afraid to hope—or to ask—for a miracle.

11

THE PROMISE: GOD IS CONSTANTLY PROVIDING OPPORTUNITIES FOR RENEWAL AND GROWTH

Remember ye not the former things, neither consider
the things of old. Behold, I will do a new thing.
ISAIAH 43:18–19 KJV

As you look at the landscape of your life, do you see opportunities, possibilities, and blessings, or do you focus, instead, upon the more negative scenery? Do you believe the Bible promise that God is making all things new—including you—or do you believe that's a promise that only applies to other people? If you've acquired the unfortunate habit of focusing too intently upon the negative aspects of your life, then your spiritual vision needs correction.

Whether you realize it or not, opportunities are whirling around you like stars crossing the night sky: beautiful to observe, but too numerous to count. Yet you may be too concerned with the challenges of everyday living to notice those opportunities. That's why you should slow down occasionally, catch your breath, and focus you thoughts on two things: the talents God has given you and the opportunities that He has placed before you. The Lord is leading you in the direction of those opportunities. Your task is to watch carefully, to pray fervently, and to act accordingly.

If you're consistently looking for the silver linings instead of the clouds, you'll discover that opportunities have a way of turning up in the most unexpected places. But if you've acquired the unfortunate habit of looking for problems instead of possibilities, you'll find that troubles have a way of turning up in unexpected places too. Since you're likely to find what you're looking for, why not look for opportunities? They're out there. And the rest is up to you.

MORE THOUGHTS ABOUT OPPORTUNITIES

We are all faced with a series of great opportunities brilliantly disguised as impossible situations.
CHARLES SWINDOLL

Each day is God's gift of a fresh unspoiled opportunity to live according to His priorities.
ELIZABETH GEORGE

The past is our teacher; the present is our opportunity; the future is our friend.
EDWIN LOUIS COLE

A possibility is a hint from God.
SØREN KIERKEGAARD

More from God's Word

But as it is written: What eye did not see and ear did not hear,
and what never entered the human mind—
God prepared this for those who love Him.
1 Corinthians 2:9 HCSB

Whenever we have the opportunity, we should do good
to everyone—especially to those in the family of faith.
Galatians 6:10 NLT

I can do all things through Christ which strengtheneth me.
Philippians 4:13 KJV

I remind you to fan into flame the gift of God.
2 Timothy 1:6 NIV

But those who wait on the Lord shall renew their strength;
they shall mount up with wings like eagles, they shall run
and not be weary, they shall walk and not faint.
Isaiah 40:31 NKJV

Remember This

God constantly arrives at our doorsteps with countless opportunities.
And He knocks. Our challenge, of course, is to open the door, to
seize the opportunity, and to receive the blessing.

12

THE PROMISE: GOD'S TIMING IS PERFECT

He has made everything appropriate in its time.
He has also put eternity in their hearts, but man cannot
discover the work God has done from beginning to end.
ECCLESIASTES 3:11 HCSB

If you're enduring difficult times, you're understandably in a hurry for things to improve. You want solutions to your problems as soon as possible, preferably today. And because you know that your time on earth is limited, you may feel a sense of urgency. So you want to find a quick resolution and move on. But God may have other plans.

Our heavenly Father, in His infinite wisdom, operates according to His own timetable, not ours. He has plans that we cannot see and purposes that we cannot know. He has created a world that unfolds according to His own schedule. Thank goodness! After all, He is omniscient; His is trustworthy; and He knows what's best for us.

If you've been waiting impatiently for the Lord to answer your prayers, it's time to put a stop to all that needless worry. You can be sure that God will answer your prayers when the time is right. You job is to keep praying—and working—until He does.

More Thoughts about God's Timing

Waiting on God brings us to
the journey's end quicker than our feet.
LETTIE COWMAN

We must learn to move according to the timetable
of the Timeless One, and to be at peace.
ELISABETH ELLIOT

The Christian's journey through life
isn't a sprint but a marathon.
BILLY GRAHAM

Teach us, O Lord, the disciplines of patience,
for to wait is often harder than to work.
PETER MARSHALL

We often hear about waiting on God,
which actually means that He is waiting
until we are ready. There is another side,
however. When we wait for God,
we are waiting until He is ready.
LETTIE COWMAN

More from God's Word

Therefore humble yourselves under the mighty hand of God,
that He may exalt you in due time.
1 PETER 5:6 NKJV

Those who trust in the LORD are like Mount Zion.
It cannot be shaken; it remains forever.
PSALM 125:1 HCSB

Yet the LORD longs to be gracious to you;
he will rise up to show you compassion. For the LORD
is a God of justice. Blessed are all who wait for him!
ISAIAH 30:18 NIV

Trust in the LORD with all your heart,
and lean not on your own understanding;
in all your ways acknowledge Him,
and He shall direct your paths.
PROVERBS 3:5–6 NKJV

To every thing there is a season,
and a time to every purpose under the heaven.
ECCLESIASTES 3:1 KJV

Remember This

God is never early or late. He's always on time. Although you don't know precisely what you need—or when you need it—He does. So trust His timing.

13

THE PROMISE: IF YOU GUARD YOUR HEART AND YOUR THOUGHTS, YOU WILL BE BLESSED

*Finally, brothers and sisters, whatever is true,
whatever is noble, whatever is right, whatever is pure,
whatever is lovely, whatever is admirable—if anything is
excellent or praiseworthy—think about such things.*

PHILIPPIANS 4:8 NIV

Your thoughts are intensely powerful things. Thoughts have the power to lift you up or drag you down; they have the power to energize you or deplete you, to inspire you to greater accomplishments or to make those accomplishments impossible.

How will you direct your thoughts today? Will you obey the words of Philippians 4:8 by dwelling upon those things that are noble and admirable? Or will you allow your thoughts to be hijacked by the negativity that seems to dominate our troubled world?

Today and every day, it's up to you to celebrate the life that God has given you by focusing your mind upon things that are excellent and praiseworthy. So form the habit of spending more time thinking about your blessings and less time fretting about your hardships. Then take time to thank the Giver of all things good for gifts that are, in truth, far too numerous to count.

MORE THOUGHTS ABOUT GUARDING YOUR HEART AND THOUGHTS

The mind is like a clock that is constantly running down. It has to be wound up daily with good thoughts.
FULTON J. SHEEN

It is the thoughts and intents of the heart that shape a person's life.
JOHN ELDREDGE

The things we think are the things that feed our souls. If we think on pure and lovely things, we shall grow pure and lovely like them; and the converse is equally true.
HANNAH WHITALL SMITH

When you think on the powerful truths of Scripture, God uses His Word to change your way of thinking.
ELIZABETH GEORGE

Your life today is a result of your thinking yesterday. Your life tomorrow will be determined by what you think today.
JOHN MAXWELL

More from God's Word

Guard your heart above all else, for it is the source of life.
PROVERBS 4:23 HCSB

Set your mind on things above, not on things on the earth.
COLOSSIANS 3:2 NKJV

*The peace of God, which surpasses
all understanding, will guard your hearts
and minds through Christ Jesus.*
PHILIPPIANS 4:7 NKJV

*And do not be conformed to this world, but be transformed by
the renewing of your mind, so that you may prove what the will
of God is, that which is good and acceptable and perfect.*
ROMANS 12:2 NASB

*For to be carnally minded is death,
but to be spiritually minded is life and peace.*
ROMANS 8:6 NKJV

A Timely Tip

If your inner voice is, in reality, your inner critic, you need to tone down the criticism now. And while you're at it, train yourself to begin thinking thoughts that are more rational, more accepting, and less judgmental. In other words, focus on the positive aspects of your life, not the negative ones. When you do, you'll be happier, healthier, and more productive.

14

THE PROMISE: JESUS OFFERS THE ULTIMATE PEACE

The peace of God, which surpasses all understanding,
will guard your hearts and minds through Christ Jesus.
PHILIPPIANS 4:7 NKJV

Peace. It's such a beautiful word. It conveys images of serenity, contentment, and freedom from the trials and tribulations of everyday existence. Peace means freedom from conflict, freedom from inner turmoil, and freedom from worry. Peace is such a beautiful concept that advertisers and marketers attempt to sell it with images of relaxed vacationers lounging on the beach or happy senior citizens celebrating on the golf course. But contrary to the implied claims of modern media, real peace, genuine peace, isn't for sale. At any price.

Have you discovered the genuine peace that can be yours through Christ? Or are you still scurrying after the illusion of peace that the world promises but cannot deliver? If you've turned things over to Jesus, you'll be blessed now and forever. So what are you waiting for? Let Him rule your heart and your thoughts, beginning now. When you do, you'll experience the peace that only He can give.

More Thoughts about Finding Peace

Deep within the center of the soul
is a chamber of peace where God lives
and where, if we will enter it and quiet all
the other sounds, we can hear His gentle whisper.
Lettie Cowman

Peace does not mean to be in a place where
there is no noise, trouble, or hard work.
Peace means to be in the midst of all
those things and still be calm in your heart.
Catherine Marshall

In the center of a hurricane there is absolute
quiet and peace. There is no safer place
than in the center of the will of God.
Corrie ten Boom

God's power is great enough for our deepest desperation.
You can go on. You can pick up the pieces and start anew.
You can face your fears. You can find peace in the rubble.
There is healing for your soul.
Suzanne Dale Ezell

Only Christ can meet the deepest needs of our world
and our hearts. Christ alone can bring lasting peace.
Billy Graham

More from God's Word

Peace I leave with you, My peace I give to you;
not as the world gives do I give to you. Let not your heart
be troubled, neither let it be afraid.
John 14:27 NKJV

He Himself is our peace.
Ephesians 2:14 NASB

But the fruit of the Spirit is love, joy, peace,
patience, kindness, goodness, faith, gentleness, self-control.
Against such things there is no law.
Galatians 5:22–23 HCSB

"I will give peace, real peace, to those far and near,
and I will heal them," says the Lord.
Isaiah 57:19 NCV

These things I have spoken to you, that in Me you
may have peace. In the world you will have tribulation;
but be of good cheer, I have overcome the world.
John 16:33 NKJV

Remember This

God's peace is available to you this very moment *if* you place absolute trust in Him. The Lord is your shepherd. Trust Him now and be blessed.

15

THE PROMISE: NOTHING IS IMPOSSIBLE FOR GOD

*Looking at them, Jesus said, "With men it is impossible,
but not with God, because all things are possible with God."*
MARK 10:27 HCSB

We live in a world of infinite possibilities. But sometimes, because of limited faith and limited understanding, we wrongly assume that God cannot or will not intervene in the affairs of mankind. Such assumptions are simply wrong.

Are you afraid to ask God to do big things in your life? If so, it's time to abandon your doubts and reclaim your faith—faith in yourself, faith in your abilities, faith in your future, and faith in your heavenly Father.

Sometimes, when we read of God's miraculous works in Biblical times, we tell ourselves, "That was then, but this is now." When we do so, we are mistaken. God is with His children "now" just as He was "then." He is right here, right now, performing miracles. And He will continue to work miracles in our lives to the extent we are willing to trust Him *and* to the extent those miracles fit into the fabric of His divine plan.

Miracles—both great and small—happen around us all day every day, but usually we're too busy to notice. Some miracles, like the twinkling of a star or the glory of a sunset, we take for granted. Other miracles, like the healing of a terminally sick patient, we chalk up to fate or to luck. We assume, quite incorrectly, that God is "out there" and we are "right here." Nothing could be further from the truth.

Do you lack the faith that God can work miracles in your own life? If so, it's time to reconsider. Instead of doubting God, trust His power and expect His miracles. Then wait patiently because something miraculous is about to happen. And it may happen sooner than you think.

MORE THOUGHTS ABOUT MIRACLES

God specializes in things thought impossible.
CATHERINE MARSHALL

God is able to do what we can't do.
BILLY GRAHAM

Are you looking for a miracle? If you keep your eyes wide open and trust in God, you won't have to look very far.
MARIE T. FREEMAN

God's specialty is raising dead things to life and making impossible things possible. You don't have the need that exceeds His power.
BETH MOORE

Miracles are not contrary to nature, but only contrary to what we know about nature.
ST. AUGUSTINE

More from God's Word

Is anything too hard for the LORD?
GENESIS 18:14 NKJV

God confirmed the message by giving
signs and wonders and various miracles
and gifts of the Holy Spirit whenever he chose.
HEBREWS 2:4 NLT

"What no eye has seen, what no ear has heard,
and what no human mind has conceived"—
the things God has prepared for those who love him—
these are the things God has revealed to us by his Spirit.
1 CORINTHIANS 2:9–10 NIV

You are the God of great wonders! You demonstrate
your awesome power among the nations.
PSALM 77:14 NLT

For with God nothing shall be impossible.
LUKE 1:37 KJV

Remember This

God has infinite power. If you're watchful, you'll observe many miracles. So keep your eyes, your mind, and your heart open.

16

The Promise: The Lord Is in Control

He is the Lord. He will do what He thinks is good.
1 Samuel 3:18 HCSB

If you're like most people, you like being in control. Period. You want things to happen according to your wishes and according to your timetable. But sometimes God has other plans, and He always has the final word.

Oswald Chambers correctly observed, "Our Lord never asks us to decide for Him; He asks us to yield to Him—a very different matter." These words remind us that even when we cannot understand the workings of God, we must trust Him and accept His will.

When Jesus went to the Mount of Olives, as described in Luke 22, He poured out His heart to God. Jesus knew of the agony that He was destined to endure, but He also knew that God's will must be done. We, like our Savior, face trials that bring fear and trembling to the very depths of our souls, but like Christ, we too must ultimately seek the Lord's will, not our own.

Are you embittered by a personal tragedy or a life-altering disappointment that you did not deserve and cannot fully understand? If so, it's time to make peace with your personal history. It's time to forgive others and, if necessary, to forgive yourself. It's time to accept the unchangeable past, to embrace the priceless present, and to have faith in the promise of tomorrow. It's time to trust God completely. And it's time to reclaim the peace—His peace—that can and should be yours.

More Thoughts about the Art of Acceptance

Christians who are strong in the faith grow as they accept whatever God allows to enter their lives.
Billy Graham

One of the marks of spiritual maturity is the quiet confidence that God is in control, without the need to understand why He does what He does.
Charles Swindoll

Loving Him means the thankful acceptance of all things that His love has appointed.
Elisabeth Elliot

Accept each day as it comes to you. Do not waste your time and energy wishing for a different set of circumstances.
Sarah Young

Acceptance says, "True, this is my situation at the moment. I'll look unblinkingly at the reality of it. But, I'll also open my hands to accept willingly whatever a loving Father sends."
Catherine Marshall

More from God's Word

*Should we accept only good things from
the hand of God and never anything bad?*
JOB 2:10 NLT

*Everything God made is good, and nothing
should be refused if it is accepted with thanks.*
1 TIMOTHY 4:4 NCV

*Trust in the LORD with all your heart
and lean not on your own understanding.*
PROVERBS 3:5 NIV

*For Yahweh is good, and His love is eternal;
His faithfulness endures through all generations.*
PSALM 100:5 HCSB

*For now we see in a mirror, dimly,
but then face to face. Now I know in part,
but then I shall know just as I also am known.*
1 CORINTHIANS 13:12 NKJV

A Timely Tip

Acceptance means learning to trust God more. Today, think of at least one aspect of your life that you've been reluctant to accept, and then prayerfully ask the Lord to help you trust Him more by accepting the past.

17

THE PROMISE: REST

*Come unto me, all ye that labour and are heavy laden,
and I will give you rest.*

MATTHEW 11:28 KJV

Even the most inspired Christians can, from time to time, find themselves running on empty. Tough times can sow seeds of doubt and fear. And the demands of daily life can drain us of our strength and rob us of the joy that is rightfully ours in Christ. When we find ourselves tired, discouraged, or worse, there is a source from which we can draw the power needed to recharge our spiritual batteries. That source is God.

The Lord intends that His children lead joyous lives filled with abundance and peace. But sometimes, abundance and peace seem very far away. It is then that we must turn to God for renewal, and when we do, He will restore us.

The world tempts you to stay up late focusing on an endless stream of media messages. But too much late-night screen time robs you of something you need very badly: sleep. So the next time you're tempted to engage in late-night time-wasting activities, resist the temptation. Instead, turn your thoughts and prayers to God. And when you're finished, turn off the lights and go to bed. You need rest more than you need entertainment.

More Thoughts about Rest

God specializes in giving people a fresh start.
RICK WARREN

The creation of a new heart,
the renewing of a right spirit is an omnipotent
work of God. Leave it to the Creator.
HENRY DRUMMOND

Are you weak? Weary? Confused? Troubled?
Pressured? How is your relationship
with God? Is it held in its place of priority?
I believe the greater the pressure,
the greater your need for time alone with Him.
KAY ARTHUR

Our Lord never drew power from Himself;
He drew it always from His Father.
OSWALD CHAMBERS

God is not running an antique shop!
He is making all things new!
VANCE HAVNER

More from God's Word

Those who hope in the LORD will renew their strength.
They will soar on wings like eagles; they will run
and not grow weary, they will walk and not be faint.
ISAIAH 40:31 NIV

I will refresh the weary and satisfy the faint.
JEREMIAH 31:25 NIV

Remember ye not the former things, neither consider
the things of old. Behold, I will do a new thing.
ISAIAH 43:18–19 KJV

Finally, brothers, rejoice. Become mature,
be encouraged, be of the same mind, be at peace,
and the God of love and peace will be with you.
2 CORINTHIANS 13:11 HCSB

Now the God of all grace, who called you
to His eternal glory in Christ Jesus, will personally restore,
establish, strengthen, and support you.
1 PETER 5:10 HCSB

A Timely Tip

If your fuse is chronically short—or if you find yourself feeling exhausted or emotionally drained or both—perhaps you need a little more sleep. So try this experiment: turn off all screens and go to bed at a reasonable hour. You'll be amazed at how good you feel when you get eight hours' sleep.

18

THE PROMISE: THE LORD SHOWERS BLESSINGS UPON THE RIGHTEOUS

Blessings crown the head of the righteous.
PROVERBS 10:6 NIV

Because we have been so richly blessed, we should make thanksgiving a habit, a regular part of our daily routines. But sometimes, amid the demands and obligations of everyday life, we may allow interruptions or distractions to interfere with the time we spend with God.

Have you counted your blessings today? And have you thanked God for them? Hopefully so. After all, His gifts include your family, your friends, your talents, your opportunities, your possessions, and the priceless gift of eternal life. These are incredible gifts, and the Lord is responsible for every one of them.

So today, as you experience the inevitable ups and downs of life here on earth, pause and give thanks to the Creator. He deserves your praise, and you deserve the experience of praising Him.

More Thoughts about God's Blessings

God's gifts put men's best dreams to shame.
ELIZABETH BARRETT BROWNING

God is always trying to give good things to us,
but our hands are too full to receive them.
ST. AUGUSTINE

It is God's will to bless us,
but not necessarily on our terms.
Sometimes what we think
would be a wonderful blessing
would not bless us at all.
JOYCE MEYER

We do not need to beg Him to bless us;
He simply cannot help it.
HANNAH WHITALL SMITH

God is the giver, and we are the receivers.
And His richest gifts are bestowed not upon those
who do the greatest things, but upon those
who accept His abundance and His grace.
HANNAH WHITALL SMITH

More from God's Word

May Yahweh bless you and protect you;
may Yahweh make His face
shine on you and be gracious to you.
NUMBERS 6:24–25 HCSB

You will show me the path of life;
in Your presence is fullness of joy;
at Your right hand are pleasures forevermore.
PSALM 16:11 NKJV

The LORD is good to all:
and his tender mercies are over all his works.
PSALM 145:9 KJV

The LORD is my rock, my fortress, and my deliverer,
my God, my mountain where I seek refuge.
My shield, the horn of my salvation,
my stronghold, my refuge, and my Savior.
2 SAMUEL 22:2–3 HCSB

The LORD is my shepherd; I shall not want.
PSALM 23:1 KJV

Remember This

God gives us countless blessings. We, in turn, should attempt to count them. And when we've counted as many as we can, we should give Him the thanks and the praise He deserves.

19

THE PROMISE: NO PROBLEMS ARE TOO BIG FOR GOD

People who do what is right may have many problems,
but the LORD will solve them all.

PSALM 34:19 NCV

Life is an adventure in problem solving. The question is not whether we will encounter problems; the real question is how we will choose to address them. When it comes to solving the problems of everyday living, we often know precisely what needs to be done, but we may be slow in doing it, especially if what needs to be done is difficult. So we put off till tomorrow what should be done today.

As a person living in the twenty-first century, you have your own set of challenges. As you face those challenges, you may be comforted by this fact: Trouble, of every kind, is temporary. Yet God's grace is eternal. And worries, of every kind, are temporary. But God's love is everlasting. The difficulties that concern you will pass. God remains. And for every problem, God has a solution.

The words of Psalm 34 remind us that the Lord solves problems for "people who do what is right." And usually, doing "what is right" means doing the uncomfortable work of confronting our problems sooner rather than later. So with no further ado, let the problem solving begin *immediately*.

MORE THOUGHTS ABOUT PROBLEM SOLVING

We are all faced with a series of great opportunities, brilliantly disguised as unsolvable problems. Unsolvable without God's wisdom, that is.
CHARLES SWINDOLL

Life will be made or broken at the place where we meet and deal with obstacles.
E. STANLEY JONES

Each problem is a God-appointed instructor.
CHARLES SWINDOLL

God is bigger than your problems. Whatever worries press upon you today, put them in God's hands and leave them there.
BILLY GRAHAM

Every problem comes gift-wrapped in a package that also contains a creative solution. When you open the package that contains the problem, the solution is there, too. Your job is to accept both gifts.
MARIE T. FREEMAN

More from God's Word

Consider it a great joy, my brothers, whenever you experience various trials, knowing that the testing of your faith produces endurance. But endurance must do its complete work, so that you may be mature and complete, lacking nothing.
James 1:2–4 HCSB

We also have joy with our troubles, because we know that these troubles produce patience. And patience produces character, and character produces hope.
Romans 5:3–4 NCV

Trust the LORD your God with all your heart and lean not on your own understanding; in all your ways acknowledge him, and he will make your paths straight.
Proverbs 3:5–6 NIV

We are pressured in every way but not crushed; we are perplexed but not in despair.
2 Corinthians 4:8 HCSB

I have learned in whatever state I am, to be content.
Philippians 4:11 NKJV

A Timely Tip

Today, think about the wisdom of tackling your problems sooner rather than later. Remember that "this, too, will pass," but whatever "it" is will pass more quickly if you spend more time solving your problems and less time fretting about them.

20

THE PROMISE: WHEN YOU LEARN TO TRUST THE LORD, YOU WILL BE CONTENT

Those who listen to instruction will prosper;
those who trust the LORD will be joyful.
PROVERBS 16:20 NLT

Do you seek happiness, abundance, and contentment? If so, here are some things you should do: love God and His Son; depend upon God's promises; try, to the best of your abilities, to follow God's will; and strive to obey His holy Word. When you do these things, you'll discover that happiness goes hand-in-hand with righteousness. The happiest people are not those who rebel against God; the happiest people are those who love God and obey His commandments.

What does life have in store for you? A world full of possibilities (of course it's up to you to seize them), and God's promise of abundance (of course it's up to you to accept it). So as you rise above your difficult circumstances and embark upon the next phase of your journey, remember to celebrate the life that God has given you. Your Creator has blessed you beyond measure. Honor Him with your prayers, your words, your deeds, and your joy.

More Thoughts
about Happiness

The practical effect of Christianity is happiness,
therefore let it be spread abroad everywhere!
C. H. Spurgeon

The truth is that even in the midst of trouble,
happy moments swim by us every day,
like shining fish waiting to be caught.
Barbara Johnson

Happy is the person who has learned the secret
of being content with whatever life brings him.
Billy Graham

Joy comes not from what we have but what we are.
C. H. Spurgeon

Happiness is a thing that comes and goes.
It can never be an end in itself.
Holiness, not happiness, is the end of man.
Oswald Chambers

More from God's Word

If they obey and serve him,
they will spend the rest of their days in
prosperity and their years in contentment.
JOB 36:11 NIV

I have come that they may have life,
and that they may have it more abundantly.
JOHN 10:10 NKJV

Happiness makes a person smile,
but sadness can break a person's spirit.
PROVERBS 15:13 NCV

A joyful heart is good medicine,
but a broken spirit dries up the bones.
PROVERBS 17:22 HCSB

Joyful is the person who finds wisdom,
the one who gains understanding.
PROVERBS 3:13 NLT

A Timely Tip

To make happiness last, we must strive to trust God's promises and to celebrate His blessings. To make happiness disappear, we need only ignore His promises and overlook His blessings.

21

THE PROMISE:
WHEN YOU BECOME A
COMPLAINT-FREE ZONE,
YOU WILL BE BLESSED

My dear brothers and sisters,
always be willing to listen and slow to speak.
JAMES 1:19 NCV

Most of us have more blessings than we can count, yet we can still find reasons to complain about the minor frustrations of everyday life. To do so, of course, is not only shortsighted, but it is also a serious roadblock on the path to spiritual abundance.

Would you like to feel more comfortable with your circumstances and your life? Then promise yourself that you'll do whatever it takes to ensure that you focus your thoughts on the major blessings you've received, not the minor inconveniences you must occasionally endure.

So the next time you're tempted to complain about the inevitable frustrations of everyday living, resist the temptation. Instead, make it a practice to count your blessings, not your hardships. It's the best way to think *and* the best way to live.

More thoughts about Becoming a Complaint-free Zone

Thanksgiving or complaining—these words
express two contrasting attitudes of the
souls of God's children. The soul that gives thanks
can find comfort in everything;
the soul that complains can find comfort in nothing.
Hannah Whitall Smith

It is always possible to be thankful for
what is given rather than to complain about what is
not given. One or the other becomes a habit of life.
Elisabeth Elliot

Don't complain. The more you
complain about things, the more things
you'll have to complain about.
E. Stanley Jones

Grumbling and gratitude are, for the child
of God, in conflict. Be grateful and you won't grumble.
Grumble and you won't be grateful.
Billy Graham

If we have our eyes upon ourselves, our problems,
and our pain, we cannot lift our eyes upward.
Billy Graham

More from God's Word

Be hospitable to one another without complaining.
1 PETER 4:9 HCSB

Do everything without complaining or arguing.
Then you will be innocent and without any wrong.
PHILIPPIANS 2:14–15 NCV

Those who guard their lips preserve their lives,
but those who speak rashly will come to ruin.
PROVERBS 13:3 NIV

A fool's displeasure is known at once,
but whoever ignores an insult is sensible.
PROVERBS 12:16 HCSB

Those who consider themselves religious
and yet do not keep a tight rein on their tongues
deceive themselves, and their religion is worthless.
JAMES 1:26 NIV

A Timely Tip

If you feel a personal pity party coming on, slow down and start counting your blessings. When you do, you'll soon discover that if you fill your heart with gratitude, there's simply no room left for complaints.

22

THE PROMISE: THE LORD CREATED YOU FOR A SPECIFIC PURPOSE

For it is God who is working in you,
enabling you both to desire
and to work out His good purpose.
PHILIPPIANS 2:13 HCSB

What did God put me here to do?" If you're like most people, you've asked yourself that question on many occasions. Perhaps you've pondered your future, uncertain of your plans, unsure of your next step. But even if you don't have a clear plan for the next step of your life's journey, you may rest assured that God does.

God has a plan for the universe, and He has a plan for you. He understands that plan as thoroughly and completely as He knows you. If you seek God's will earnestly and prayerfully, He will make His plans known to you in His own time and in His own way.

Do you sincerely seek to discover God's purpose for your life? If so, you must be willing to live in accordance with His commandments. You must also study God's Word and be watchful for His signs.

Finally, you must ask for God's guidance every day—beginning with this one—and you must have faith that He will eventually reveal His plans to you.

Perhaps your vision of God's purpose for your life has been clouded by a wish list that you have expected God to dutifully fulfill. Perhaps you have fervently hoped that God would create a world that unfolds according to your wishes, not His. If so, you have experienced more disappointment than satisfaction and more frustration than peace. A better strategy is to conform your will to God's (and not to struggle vainly in an attempt to conform His will to yours).

Sometimes God's plans and purposes may seem unmistakably clear to you. If so, push ahead. But other times He may lead you through the wilderness before He directs you to the Promised Land. So be patient and keep seeking His will for your life. When you do, you'll be amazed at the marvelous things that an all-powerful, all-knowing God can do.

MORE THOUGHTS ABOUT DISCOVERING PURPOSE

*The easiest way to discover the purpose of an invention
is to ask the creator of it. The same is true
for discovering your life's purpose: Ask God.*
RICK WARREN

*You weren't an accident. You weren't mass produced.
You aren't an assembly-line product.
You were deliberately planned, specifically gifted, and lovingly
positioned on the earth by the Master Craftsman.*
MAX LUCADO

There's some task which the God
of all the universe, the great Creator
has for you to do, and which will remain
undone and incomplete, until by faith
and obedience, you step into the will of God.
ALAN REDPATH

All of God's people are ordinary people
who have been made extraordinary
by the purpose He has given them.
OSWALD CHAMBERS

Live out your life in its full meaning; it is God's life.
JOSIAH ROYCE

MORE FROM GOD'S WORD

We have also received an inheritance in Him,
predestined according to the purpose of
the One who works out everything in
agreement with the decision of His will.
EPHESIANS 1:11 HCSB

So whether you eat or drink,
or whatever you do, do it all for the glory of God.
1 CORINTHIANS 10:31 NLT

For we are God's coworkers.
You are God's field, God's building.
1 CORINTHIANS 3:9 HCSB

For we are His creation, created in Christ Jesus
for good works, which God prepared
ahead of time so that we should walk in them.
EPHESIANS 2:10 HCSB

We must do the works of Him
who sent Me while it is day.
Night is coming when no one can work.
JOHN 9:4 HCSB

A TIMELY TIP

Perhaps you're in a hurry to understand God's unfolding plan for your life. If so, remember that God operates according to a perfect timetable. That timetable is His, not yours. So be patient. God has big things in store for you, but He may have quite a few lessons to teach you before you are fully prepared to do His will and fulfill His purpose.

23

THE PROMISE: WHEN YOU STUDY GOD'S WORD, YOU'LL BE BLESSED

*All Scripture is given by inspiration of God,
and is profitable for doctrine, for reproof,
for correction, for instruction in righteousness.*
2 TIMOTHY 3:16 KJV

Is Bible study a high priority for you? The answer to this simple question will determine, to a surprising extent, the quality and direction of your life.

As you deal with difficult times and establish priorities, you must decide whether God's Word will be a bright spotlight that guides your path every day or a tiny night-light that occasionally flickers in the dark. The decision to study the Bible—or not—is yours and yours alone. But make no mistake: how you choose to use your Bible will have a profound impact on you and your loved ones.

George Mueller observed, "The vigor of our spiritual lives will be in exact proportion to the place held by the Bible in our lives and in our thoughts." Think of it like this: the more you use your Bible, the more God will use you.

God's Word can be a roadmap to a place of peace and abundance. Make it your roadmap. God's wisdom can be a light to guide your steps. Claim it as your light today, tomorrow, and every day of your life.

MORE THOUGHTS ABOUT BIBLE STUDY

Reading the Bible has a purifying effect upon your life.
Let nothing take the place of this daily exercise.
BILLY GRAHAM

Gather the riches of God's promises.
Nobody can take away from you those
texts from the Bible which you have learned by heart.
CORRIE TEN BOOM

Read the Scripture, not only as history,
but as a love letter sent to you from God.
THOMAS WATSON

I believe the reason so many are
failing today is that they have not
disciplined themselves to read
God's Word consistently, day in and day out,
and to apply it to every situation in life.
KAY ARTHUR

Do you want your faith to grow?
Then let the Bible began to saturate your mind and soul.
BILLY GRAHAM

More from God's Word

The counsel of the LORD stands forever,
the plans of His heart from generation to generation.
PSALM 33:11 NASB

But the word of the Lord endures forever.
And this is the word that was
preached as the gospel to you.
1 PETER 1:25 HCSB

But whoever looks intently into the perfect law that gives
freedom, and continues in it—not forgetting what they have
heard, but doing it—they will be blessed in what they do.
JAMES 1:25 NIV

But grow in the grace and knowledge
of our Lord and Savior Jesus Christ.
To Him be the glory both now and to the day of eternity.
2 PETER 3:18 HCSB

You will be a good servant of Christ Jesus,
nourished by the words of the faith
and of the good teaching that you have followed.
1 TIMOTHY 4:6 HCSB

Remember This

You're never too young—or too old—to become a serious student of God's Word. If you're not already reading your Bible every day, the appropriate time to begin is now.

24

THE PROMISE: THE LORD WANTS YOU TO REJOICE

Rejoice in the Lord always. Again I will say, rejoice!
PHILIPPIANS 4:4 NKJV

Today is a nonrenewable resource—once it's gone, it's gone forever. Our responsibility, as thoughtful believers, is to use this day in the service of God's will and in the service of His people. When we do so, we enrich our own lives and the lives of the people we love.

Oswald Chambers correctly observed, "Joy is the great note all throughout the Bible." E. Stanley Jones echoed that thought when he wrote, "Christ and joy go together." But even the most dedicated Christians can, on occasion, forget that each day is a priceless gift from the Creator.

What do you expect from the day ahead? Are you expecting God to do wonderful things, or are you living beneath a cloud of apprehension and doubt? The familiar words of Psalm 118:24 remind us of a profound yet simple truth: "This is the day which the LORD hath made" (KJV). Our duty, as believers, is to rejoice in God's marvelous creation.

Today, celebrate the life that God has given you. Today, put a smile on your face, kind words on your lips, and a song in your heart.

Be generous with your praise and free with your encouragement. And then, when you have celebrated life to the full, invite your friends to do likewise. After all, this is God's day, and He has given us clear instructions for its use. We are commanded to rejoice and be glad. So with no further ado, let the celebration begin…

MORE THOUGHTS
ABOUT CELEBRATION

God knows everything. He can manage everything,
and He loves us. Surely this is enough
for a fullness of joy that is beyond words.
HANNAH WHITALL SMITH

Every day we live is a priceless gift of God, loaded with
possibilities to learn something new, to gain fresh insights.
DALE EVANS ROGERS

There is not one blade of grass, there is no color
in this world that is not intended to make us rejoice.
JOHN CALVIN

All our life is celebration to us. We are convinced,
in fact, that God is always everywhere.
ST. CLEMENT OF ALEXANDRIA

The greatest honor you can give Almighty God is to live
gladly and joyfully because of the knowledge of His love.
JULIAN OF NORWICH

More from God's Word

A happy heart is like a continual feast.
PROVERBS 15:15 NCV

*I have spoken these things to you so that My joy
may be in you and your joy may be complete.*
JOHN 15:11 HCSB

*Rejoice always, pray without ceasing,
in everything give thanks; for this is the
will of God in Christ Jesus for you.*
1 THESSALONIANS 5:16–18 NKJV

*I delight greatly in the LORD;
my soul rejoices in my God.*
ISAIAH 61:10 NIV

*I came that they may have life,
and have it abundantly.*
JOHN 10:10 NASB

A Timely Tip

Every new day should be a cause for celebration. By celebrating the
gift of life, you protect your heart from the dangers of pessimism,
regret, hopelessness, and bitterness.

25

THE PROMISE:
WORSHIP CAN, AND SHOULD,
BE A JOYFUL EXPERIENCE

I was glad when they said unto me,
Let us go into the house of the LORD.
PSALM 122:1 KJV

To worship God is a privilege, but it's a privilege that far too many of us forego. Instead of praising our Creator seven days a week, we worship Him on Sunday mornings (if at all) and spend the rest of the week focusing on other things. And when difficult times arrive, we may become so consumed by worry and doubt that we fail to worship the Lord "in spirit and in truth."

Whenever we become distracted by worldly pursuits that put God in second place, we inevitably pay a price for our misplaced priorities. A better strategy, of course, is to worship the Lord every day of the week, beginning with a regular early morning devotional.

Every new day provides us with another opportunity to experience the joy of worship. And each day offers another chance to support God's church and serve God's children. When we do so, we bless others, and we are blessed by the One who sent His only begotten Son so that we might have eternal life.

More Thoughts about Worship

Worship is an inward reverence,
the bowing down of the soul in the presence of God.
Elizabeth George

Worship in the truest sense takes place
only when our full attention is on God—
His glory, majesty, love, and compassion.
Billy Graham

Worship is focus.
Beth Moore

We must worship in truth.
Worship is not just an emotional
exercise but a response of the heart
built on truth about God.
Erwin Lutzer

Even the most routine part of your
day can be a spiritual act of worship.
Sarah Young

MORE FROM GOD'S WORD

God is Spirit, and those who worship Him
must worship in spirit and truth.
JOHN 4:24 HCSB

Happy are those who hear the joyful call to worship,
for they will walk in
the light of your presence, LORD.
PSALM 89:15 NLT

All the earth will worship You and sing praise to You.
They will sing praise to Your name.
PSALM 66:4 HCSB

For where two or three are gathered together
in My name, I am there among them.
MATTHEW 18:20 HCSB

Worship the LORD with gladness. Come before him, singing
with joy. Acknowledge that the LORD is God! He made us,
and we are his. We are his people, the sheep of his pasture.
PSALM 100:2–3 NLT

A TIMELY TIP

Worship reminds you of the awesome power of God. So worship Him daily, and allow Him to work through you every day of the week (not just on Sunday morning). And please remember that the best way to worship God is to worship Him sincerely and often.

26

THE PROMISE: MATERIALISM IS DANGEROUS

*Do not love the world or the things that belong
to the world. If anyone loves the world,
love for the Father is not in him.*

1 JOHN 2:15 HCSB

In our demanding world, financial prosperity can be a good thing, but spiritual prosperity is profoundly more important. Certainly we all need the basic necessities of life, but inevitably the piling up of possessions creates more problems than it solves. Our real riches, of course, are not of this world. We are never really rich until we are rich in spirit. Yet we live in a society that leads us to believe otherwise. The media often glorifies material possessions above all else; God most certainly does not.

Martin Luther observed, "Many things I have tried to grasp and have lost. That which I have placed in God's hands I still have." His words apply to all of us. Our earthly riches are transitory; our spiritual riches, on the other hand, are everlasting.

Do you find yourself wrapped up in the concerns of the material world? If so, it's time to reorder your priorities and reassess your values. And then, it's time to begin storing up riches that will endure throughout eternity: the spiritual kind.

MORE THOUGHTS ABOUT MATERIALISM

It's sobering to contemplate how much time, effort, sacrifice, compromise, and attention we give to acquiring and increasing our supply of something that is totally insignificant in eternity.
ANNE GRAHAM LOTZ

Where the soul is full of peace and joy, outward surroundings and circumstances are of comparatively little account.
HANNAH WHITALL SMITH

Contentment is possible when we stop striving for more.
CHARLES SWINDOLL

Possessions only provide temporary happiness.
RICK WARREN

What we possess often possesses us— we are possessed by possessions.
OSWALD CHAMBERS

More from God's Word

*No one can serve two masters. For you will hate one and love
the other; you will be devoted to one and despise the other. You
cannot serve God and be enslaved to money.*
LUKE 16:13 NLT

For where your treasure is, there your heart will be also.
LUKE 12:34 HCSB

*Your life should be free from the love of money.
Be satisfied with what you have, for He Himself has said,
I will never leave you or forsake you.*
HEBREWS 13:5 HCSB

*We brought nothing into the world, so we can take nothing out.
But, if we have food and clothes, we will be satisfied with that.*
1 TIMOTHY 6:7–8 NCV

*There is one who makes himself rich, yet has nothing;
and one who makes himself poor, yet has great riches.*
PROVERBS 13:7 NKJV

Remember This

The world wants you to believe that money can buy happiness. Don't
believe it! Genuine happiness comes not from money or the things
that money can buy. Genuine happiness flows from the things that
money cannot buy, starting, of course, with your relationship to God
and His only begotten Son.

27

THE PROMISE: WHEN TIMES ARE TOUGH, THE LORD IS YOUR REFUGE

God is our protection and our strength.
He always helps in times of trouble.
PSALM 46:1 NCV

You've probably heard it said on many occasions. Perhaps you've even said it yourself: "I'm doing the best I can *under the circumstances*." But God has a better way. He wants you to live *above* your circumstances—and with His help, you can most certainly do it.

In his letter to the Philippians, Paul stated that he could find happiness and fulfillment in any situation (Philippians 4:11). How? By turning his life and his future over to the Lord. Even when he faced enormous difficulties, Paul found peace through God. So can you.

Today, make this important promise to yourself and to your Creator: Promise to rise far above your circumstances. You deserve no less, and neither, for that matter, does your Father in heaven.

More Thoughts about Dealing with Difficult Circumstances

No matter what our circumstance,
we can find a reason to be thankful.
DAVID JEREMIAH

God has a purpose behind every problem.
He uses circumstances to develop our character.
In fact, He depends more on circumstances
to make us like Jesus than He
depends on our reading the Bible.
RICK WARREN

Don't let obstacles along the road to eternity
shake your confidence in God's promises.
DAVID JEREMIAH

Every experience God gives us, every person
He brings into our lives, is the perfect preparation
for the future that only He can see.
CORRIE TEN BOOM

Oftentimes God demonstrates His faithfulness
in adversity by providing for us what we need
to survive. He does not change our painful
circumstances. He sustains us through them.
CHARLES STANLEY

More from God's Word

I have learned in whatever state I am, to be content.
PHILIPPIANS 4:11 NKJV

Trust in him at all times, you people;
pour out your hearts to him, for God is our refuge.
PSALM 62:8 NIV

The LORD is a refuge for His people and a stronghold.
JOEL 3:16 NASB

The LORD is a refuge for the oppressed,
a refuge in times of trouble.
PSALM 9:9 HCSB

Cast your burden on the LORD,
and He shall sustain you;
He shall never permit the righteous to be moved.
PSALM 55:22 NKJV

Remember This

A change of circumstances is rarely as important as a change in attitude. If you change your thoughts, you will most certainly change your circumstances.

28

THE PROMISE: WHEN YOU FORGIVE OTHERS, YOU WILL BE FORGIVEN AND YOU WILL BE BLESSED

Judge not, and you shall not be judged. Condemn not, and you shall not be condemned. Forgive, and you will be forgiven.

LUKE 6:37 NKJV

When we have been injured or embarrassed, we feel the urge to strike back and to hurt the ones who have hurt us. But Christ instructs us to do otherwise. Christ teaches us that forgiveness is God's way and that mercy is an integral part of God's plan for our lives. In short, we are commanded to weave the thread of forgiveness into the very fabric of our lives.

Do you invest more time than you should focusing on past injustices? Are you troubled by feelings of anger, bitterness, envy, or regret? Do you harbor ill will against someone you simply can't seem to forgive? If so, it's time to finally get serious about forgiveness.

When someone hurts you, the act of forgiveness is difficult but necessary. Until you forgive, you are trapped in a prison of your own creation. But what if you have tried to forgive and simply can't seem to do so? The solution to your dilemma is this: you simply must make forgiveness a higher priority in your life.

Most of us don't spend much time thinking about forgiveness; we worry, instead, about the injustices we have suffered and the people who inflicted them. But God wants us to live in the present, not the past, and He knows that in order to do so, we must forgive those who have harmed us.

Have you made forgiveness a high priority? And have you sincerely asked God to help you forgive others? If so, congratulations. If not, perhaps it's time to rearrange your priorities. And perhaps it's time to improve your life by freeing yourself, once and for all, from the chains of bitterness, regret, and unresolved anger.

More Thoughts about Forgiveness

As you have received the mercy of God by the forgiveness of sin and the promise of eternal life, thus you must show mercy.
Billy Graham

To be a Christian means to forgive the inexcusable, because God has forgiven the inexcusable in you.
C. S. Lewis

There is always room for more loving forgiveness within our homes.
James Dobson

Learning how to forgive and forget is one of the secrets of a happy Christian life.
Warren Wiersbe

More from God's Word

Above all, love each other deeply,
because love covers a multitude of sins.
1 PETER 4:8 NIV

But I say to you, love your enemies
and pray for those who persecute you.
MATTHEW 5:44 NASB

And be kind to one another, tenderhearted,
forgiving one another,
just as God in Christ forgave you.
EPHESIANS 4:32 NKJV

And whenever you stand praying,
if you have anything against anyone,
forgive him, so that your Father in heaven
will also forgive you your wrongdoing.
MARK 11:25 HCSB

The merciful are blessed, for they will be shown mercy.
MATTHEW 5:7 HCSB

A Timely Tip

Today, make a list of the people you still need to forgive. Then make up your mind to forgive at least one person on that list. Finally, ask God to cleanse your heart of bitterness, animosity, and regret. If you ask Him sincerely and often, He will respond.

29

THE PROMISE: RENEWAL

You are being renewed in the spirit of your minds;
you put on the new self, the one created according to God's
likeness in righteousness and purity of the truth.
EPHESIANS 4:23–24 HCSB

For busy citizens of the twenty-first century, it's easy to become overcommitted, overworked, and overstressed. If we choose, we can be connected 24/7, sparing just enough time for a few hours' sleep each night. What we need is time to renew and recharge, but where can we find the time? We can—and should—find it with God.

The Lord can renew your strength and restore your spirits if you let Him. But He won't force you to slow down, and He won't insist that you get enough sleep at night. He leaves those choices up to you.

If you're feeling chronically tired or discouraged, it's time to rearrange your schedule, turn off the TV, power down the phone, and spend quiet time with your Creator. He knows what you need, and He wants you to experience His peace and His love. He's ready, willing, and perfectly able to renew your strength and help you prioritize the items on your do-list if you ask Him. In fact, He's ready to hear your prayers right now. Please don't make Him wait.

More Thoughts about Renewal

Troubles we bear trustfully can bring us a fresh vision of God and a new outlook on life, an outlook of peace and hope.
BILLY GRAHAM

Walking with God leads to receiving His intimate counsel, and counseling leads to deep restoration.
JOHN ELDREDGE

The same voice that brought Lazarus out of the tomb raised us to newness of life.
C. H. SPURGEON

When we reach the end of our strength, wisdom, and personal resources, we enter into the beginning of His glorious provisions.
PATSY CLAIRMONT

He is the God of wholeness and restoration.
STORMIE OMARTIAN

More from God's Word

Therefore, if anyone is in Christ, he is a new creation; old things have passed away; behold, all things have become new.
2 CORINTHIANS 5:17 NKJV

Finally, brothers, rejoice.
Become mature, be encouraged,
be of the same mind, be at peace,
and the God of love and peace will be with you.
2 CORINTHIANS 13:11 HCSB

Now the God of all grace, who called you to
His eternal glory in Christ Jesus, will personally restore,
establish, strengthen, and support you.
1 PETER 5:10 HCSB

Remember ye not the former things,
neither consider the things of old.
Behold, I will do a new thing.
ISAIAH 43:18–19 KJV

Those who hope in the LORD will renew their strength.
They will soar on wings like eagles;
they will run and not grow weary,
they will walk and not be faint.
ISAIAH 40:31 NIV

REMEMBER THIS

God can make all things new, including you. When you are weak or worried, He can renew your spirit and restore your strength. Your job, of course, is to let Him.

30

THE PROMISE: GOD IS ALWAYS WORKING FOR THE GOOD OF THOSE WHO LOVE HIM

We know that all things work together
for the good of those who love God:
those who are called according to His purpose.

ROMANS 8:28 HCSB

Do you value your relationship with God, and do you tell Him so many times each day? Hopefully so. But if you find yourself overwhelmed by the demands of difficult times, you may find yourself scurrying from place to place with scarcely a spare moment to think about your relationship with the Creator. If so, you're simply too busy—or too distracted—for your own good.

God calls each of us to worship Him, to obey His commandments, and to accept His Son as our Savior. When we do, God blesses us in ways that we can scarcely understand. But when we allow the demands of the day to interfere with our communications with the

Father, we unintentionally distance ourselves from our greatest source of abundance and peace.

C. S. Lewis observed, "A man's spiritual health is exactly proportional to his love for God." If we are to enjoy the spiritual health that God intends for us, we must praise Him, we must love Him, and we must obey Him.

When we worship the Lord faithfully and obediently, we invite His love into our hearts. When we truly worship God, we allow Him to rule over our days and our lives. In turn, we grow to love Him more deeply as we sense His love for us.

St. Augustine wrote, "I love You, Lord, not doubtingly, but with absolute certainty. Your Word beat upon my heart until I fell in love with You, and now the universe and everything in it tells me to love You." Today, open your heart to the Father. Make yourself His dutiful servant as you follow in the footsteps of His only begotten Son. And let your obedience to the Father be a fitting response to His never-ending love for you.

More Thoughts about Loving God

When God speaks to us,
He should have our full attention.
BILLY GRAHAM

Deep within the center of the soul is a chamber
of peace where God lives and where,
if we will enter it and quiet all the other sounds,
we can hear His gentle whisper.
LETTIE COWMAN

Prayer begins by talking to God,
but it ends in listening to Him.
In the face of Absolute Truth,
silence is the soul's language.

FULTON J. SHEEN

God's voice is still and quiet and easily buried
under an avalanche of clamor.

CHARLES STANLEY

If you, too, will learn to wait upon God,
to get alone with Him, and remain silent
so that you can hear His voice when
He is ready to speak to you, what a difference
it will make in your life!

KAY ARTHUR

MORE FROM GOD'S WORD

He said to him, "Love the Lord your God
with all your heart, with all your soul,
and with all your mind. This is the greatest
and most important command."

MATTHEW 22:37–38 HCSB

We love him, because he first loved us.

1 JOHN 4:19 KJV

This is love for God: to obey his commands.
1 JOHN 5:3 NIV

*God is Spirit, and those who worship Him
must worship in spirit and truth.*
JOHN 4:24 HCSB

*I love the LORD, for he heard my voice;
he heard my cry for mercy.*
PSALM 116:1 NIV

A TIMELY TIP

If you sincerely love God, don't be too bashful to tell Him so. And while you're at it, don't be too bashful to tell other people about your feelings. If you love the Lord, say so loudly and often.

THE PROMISE: YOUR VALUES MATTER

The righteousness of the blameless clears his path,
but the wicked person will fall because of his wickedness.
PROVERBS 11:5 HCSB

Whether you realize it or not, your life is shaped by your values. From the time your alarm clock wakes you in the morning until the moment you lay your head on the pillow at night, your actions are guided by the values that you hold most dear. If you're a thoughtful believer, then those values are shaped by the Word of God.

Society seeks to impose its set of values upon you; however, these values are often contrary to God's Word (and thus contrary to your own best interests). The world makes promises that it simply cannot fulfill. It promises happiness, contentment, prosperity, and abundance. But genuine abundance is not a byproduct of possessions or status; it is a byproduct of your thoughts, your actions, and your relationship with the Lord. The world's promises are incomplete and deceptive; God's promises are unfailing. Your challenge, then, is to build your value system upon the firm foundation of God's promises. Nothing else will suffice.

Are you trying to overcome difficult circumstances? If so, then you must build your life upon a value system that puts God first. So when you're faced with a tough decision or a powerful temptation, seek God's counsel and trust the counsel that He gives. Invite Him into your heart and live according to His commandments. Study His Word and talk to Him often. When you do, you will share in the abundance and peace that only He can give.

More Thoughts about Values That Matter

Sadly, family problems and even financial problems are seldom the real problem, but often the symptom of a weak or nonexistent value system.
Dave Ramsey

If you want to be proactive in the way you live your life, if you want to influence your life's direction, if you want your life to exhibit the qualities you find desirable, and if you want to live with integrity, then you need to know what your values are, decide to embrace them, and practice them every day.
John Maxwell

Whether you have twenty years left, ten years, one year, one month, one day, or just one hour, there is something very important God wants you to do that can add to His kingdom and your blessing.
Bill Bright

Our life pursuits will reflect our character and personal integrity.
Franklin Graham

More from God's Word

So I strive always to keep my conscience
clear before God and man.
ACTS 24:16 NIV

Let us come near to God with a sincere heart and a sure faith,
because we have been made free from a guilty conscience, and
our bodies have been washed with pure water.
HEBREWS 10:22 NCV

If then you were raised with Christ, seek those things which are
above, where Christ is, sitting at the right hand of God. Set
your mind on things above, not on things on the earth.
COLOSSIANS 3:1-2 NKJV

Do not conform to the pattern of this world, but be transformed
by the renewing of your mind. Then you will be able to test and
approve what God's will is—his good, pleasing and perfect will.
ROMANS 12:2 NIV

The integrity of the upright guides them,
but the perversity of the treacherous destroys them.
PROVERBS 11:3 HCSB

Remember This

You can have the values that the world holds dear, or you can have the values that God holds dear, but you can't have both. The decision is yours, and so are the consequences.

32

THE PROMISE: FAILURE ISN'T FINAL

One who listens to life-giving rebukes
will be at home among the wise.
PROVERBS 15:31 HCSB

Life's occasional setbacks are simply the price that we must pay for our willingness to take risks as we follow our dreams. But even when we encounter bitter disappointments, we must never lose faith.

Hebrews 10:36 advises, "Patient endurance is what you need now, so that you will continue to do God's will. Then you will receive all that he has promised" (NLT). These words remind us that when we persevere, we will eventually receive the rewards God has promised. What's required is perseverance, not perfection.

When we face hardships, God stands ready to protect us. Our responsibility, of course, is to ask Him for protection. When we call upon Him in heartfelt prayer, He will answer—in His own time and according to His own plan—and He will do His part to heal us. We, of course, must do our part too.

And while we are waiting for God's plans to unfold and for His healing touch to restore us, we can be comforted in the knowledge that our Creator can overcome any obstacle, even if we cannot.

More Thoughts about Failure

*The enemy of our souls loves to taunt us with
past failures, wrongs, disappointments,
disasters, and calamities. And if we let him
continue doing this, our life becomes
a long and dark tunnel, with very little light at the end.*
Charles Swindoll

*What may seem defeat to us
may be victory to Him.*
C. H. Spurgeon

*Success or failure can be pretty well predicted
by the degree to which the heart is fully in it.*
John Eldredge

*Never imagine that you can
be a loser by trusting in God.*
C. H. Spurgeon

*Goals are worth setting and worth missing.
We learn from non-successes.*
Bill Bright

More from God's Word

Though the righteous fall seven times, they rise again.
PROVERBS 24:16 NIV

The LORD is near to those who have a broken heart.
PSALM 34:18 NKJV

If you listen to correction to improve your life,
you will live among the wise.
PROVERBS 15:31 NCV

We are hard-pressed on every side, yet not crushed;
we are perplexed, but not in despair.
2 CORINTHIANS 4:8 NKJV

But as for you, be strong; don't be discouraged,
for your work has a reward.
2 CHRONICLES 15:7 HCSB

Remember This

Failure isn't permanent *unless* you fail to get up. So pick yourself up, dust yourself off, and trust God. He will make it right. Warren Wiersbe had this advice: "No matter how badly we have failed, we can always get up and begin again. Our God is the God of new beginnings." And don't forget: the best time to begin again is now.

33

THE PROMISE
OF ABUNDANCE

I have come that they may have life,
and that they may have it more abundantly.
JOHN 10:10 NKJV

The Bible promises that God's abundance is available to each of us. He offers His blessings, but He doesn't force them upon us. To receive them, we must trust His promises and we must follow, as closely as we can, in the footsteps of His Son. But the world tempts us to do otherwise. The world tempts us to descend into fits of pessimism and doubt. And the world also bombards us with a never-ending assortment of time-squandering distractions and wallet-draining temptations.

Everywhere you turn, someone or something is vying for your attention, trying to convince you that peace and happiness are commodities that can be purchased for the right price. But buyer beware. Genuine peace and spiritual abundance are not for sale at any price. Real abundance is never obtained through worldly possessions. It results from your relationship with God.

Do you sincerely seek the abundant life that Jesus promises in John 10:10? Then turn your life and your heart over to Him. When you do, you'll receive the love, the peace, and the abundance that that can only come from the touch of the Master's hand.

More Thoughts about Abundance

God loves you and wants you to experience peace and life—abundant and eternal.
BILLY GRAHAM

God is the giver, and we are the receivers. And His richest gifts are bestowed not upon those who do the greatest things, but upon those who accept His abundance and His grace.
HANNAH WHITALL SMITH

We honor God by asking for great things when they are a part of His promise. We dishonor Him and cheat ourselves when we ask for molehills where He has promised mountains.
VANCE HAVNER

Knowing that your future is absolutely assured can free you to live abundantly today.
SARAH YOUNG

Jesus wants Life for us; Life with a capital L.
JOHN ELDREDGE

More from God's Word

Until now you have asked for nothing in My name.
Ask and you will receive, so that your joy may be complete.
JOHN 16:24 HCSB

And God is able to make all grace abound to you,
so that always having all sufficiency in everything,
you may have an abundance for every good deed.
2 CORINTHIANS 9:8 NASB

Success, success to you, and success to those
who help you, for your God will help you.
1 CHRONICLES 12:18 NIV

My cup runs over. Surely goodness and mercy
shall follow me all the days of my life;
and I will dwell in the house of the LORD forever.
PSALM 23:5–6 NKJV

May Yahweh bless you and protect you; may Yahweh
make His face shine on you and be gracious to you.
NUMBERS 6:24–25 HCSB

Remember This

Jesus came to this earth so that we might experience life abundant and life eternal. Our task, of course, is to pray, to work, to obey, and to accept His abundance with open arms.

34

THE PROMISE: YOU CAN CONTROL YOUR EMOTIONS

*For this very reason, make every effort to supplement
your faith with goodness, goodness with knowledge,
knowledge with self-control, self-control
with endurance, endurance with godliness.*

2 PETER 1:5–6 HCSB

Hebrews 10:38 teaches us, "The just shall live by faith" (NKJV). Yet sometimes, despite our best intentions, negative feelings can rob us of the peace and abundance that would otherwise be ours through Christ. When anger or anxiety separates us from the spiritual blessings that God has in store, we must rethink our priorities and renew our faith. And we must place faith above feelings.

Human emotions are highly variable, decidedly unpredictable, and often unreliable. Our emotions are like the weather, only far more fickle. So we must learn to live by faith, not by the ups and downs of our own emotional roller coasters.

Sometime during this day, you may be gripped by a strong negative emotion. Distrust it. Rein it in. Test it. And turn it over to

God. Your emotions will inevitably change; God will not. So trust Him completely as you watch your negative feelings slowly evaporate into thin air—which, of course, they will.

More Thoughts about Dealing with Emotions

Don't bother much about your feelings. When they are humble, loving, brave, give thanks for them; when they are conceited, selfish, cowardly, ask to have them altered. In neither case are they you, but only a thing that happens to you. What matters is your intentions and your behavior.
C. S. Lewis

A life lived in God is not lived on the plane of feelings, but of the will.
Elisabeth Elliot

I may no longer depend on pleasant impulses to bring me before the Lord. I must rather respond to principles I know to be right, whether I feel them to be enjoyable or not.
Jim Elliot

If you desire to improve your physical well-being and your emotional outlook, increasing your faith can help you.
John Maxwell

I do not need to feel good or be ecstatic in order to be in the center of God's will.
Bill Bright

More from God's Word

Grow a wise heart—you'll do yourself a favor;
keep a clear head—you'll find a good life.
PROVERBS 19:8 MSG

Enthusiasm without knowledge is not good.
If you act too quickly, you might make a mistake.
PROVERBS 19:2 NCV

And let the peace of God rule in your hearts, to which
also you were called in one body; and be thankful.
COLOSSIANS 3:15 NKJV

Get wisdom—how much better it is than gold!
And get understanding—it is preferable to silver.
PROVERBS 16:16 HCSB

All bitterness, anger and wrath, shouting and slander
must be removed from you, along with all malice.
And be kind and compassionate to one another, forgiving
one another, just as God also forgave you in Christ.
EPHESIANS 4:31–32 HCSB

Remember This

Your life shouldn't be ruled by your emotions—your life should be ruled by God. So if you think you've lost control over your emotions, don't make big decisions, don't strike out against anybody, and don't speak out in anger. Count to ten (or more) and take "time out" from your situation until you've managed to say a silent prayer and calm yourself down.

35

THE PROMISE: WHEN YOU
ASK GOD FOR WISDOM,
HE WILL GIVE IT

*But if any of you needs wisdom, you should
ask God for it. He is generous to everyone
and will give you wisdom without criticizing you.*

JAMES 1:5 NCV

Life is a series of choices. From the instant we wake in the morning
until the moment we nod off to sleep at night, we make countless
decisions: decisions about the things we do, decisions about the words
we speak, and decisions about the thoughts we choose to think. Simply
put, the quality of those decisions determines the quality of our lives.

As believers who have been saved by a loving and merciful God,
we have every reason to make wise choices. Yet sometimes, amid
the inevitable challenges of life here on earth, we allow ourselves to
behave in ways that we know are displeasing to our Creator. When
we do, we forfeit the joy and the peace that we might otherwise
experience through Him.

As you take the next step in your life's journey, take time to
consider how many things in this life you can control: your thoughts,

your words, your priorities, and your actions, for starters. And then, if you sincerely want to discover God's purpose for your life, make choices that are pleasing to Him. He deserves no less, and neither, for that matter do you.

More Thoughts about Making Wise Choices

Life is a series of choices between the bad, the good, and the best. Everything depends on how we choose.
Vance Havner

Every day, I find countless opportunities to decide whether I will obey God and demonstrate my love for Him or try to please myself or the world system. God is waiting for my choices.
Bill Bright

We are either the masters or the victims of our attitudes. It is a matter of personal choice. Who we are today is the result of choices we made yesterday. Tomorrow, we will become what we choose today. To change means to choose to change.
John Maxwell

The choices of time are binding in eternity.
Jack MacArthur

Get into the habit of dealing with God about everything.
Oswald Chambers

More from God's Word

In every way be an example of doing good deeds.
When you teach, do it with honesty and seriousness.
TITUS 2:7 NCV

We can make our own plans, but the LORD gives
the right answer. People may be pure in their own eyes,
but the LORD examines their motives.
PROVERBS 16:1–2 NLT

Blessed is the man who walks not in the counsel
of the ungodly, nor stands in the path of sinners,
nor sits in the seat of the scornful.
PSALM 1:1 NKJV

The highway of the upright avoids evil;
the one who guards his way protects his life.
PROVERBS 16:17 HCSB

By their fruits ye shall know them.
MATTHEW 7:20 KJV

A Timely Tip

Today, take time to think carefully about the direction of your life
and the choices that you've been making. Then try to come up with
at least one "new and improved" choice that you can make before
the end of the day.

36

THE PROMISE:
GOD REWARDS PATIENCE

The LORD is good to those who depend on him,
to those who search for him.
So it is good to wait quietly for salvation from the LORD.
LAMENTATIONS 3:25–26 NLT

The dictionary defines the word patience as "the ability to be calm, tolerant, and understanding." If that describes you, you can skip the rest of this page. But if you're like most of us, you'd better keep reading.

For most of us, patience is a hard thing to master. Why? Because we have lots of things we want, and we know precisely when we want them: *now.* But our Father in heaven has other ideas; the Bible teaches that we must learn to wait patiently for the things that God has in store for us, even when waiting is difficult.

We live in an imperfect world inhabited by imperfect people. Sometimes we inherit troubles from others, and sometimes we create troubles for ourselves. On other occasions, we see other people "moving ahead" in the world, and we want to move ahead with them. So we become impatient with ourselves and our circumstances.

Sometimes patience is the price we must pay for being responsible adults, and that's as it should be. After all, think how patient our heavenly Father has been with us. So the next time you find yourself drumming your fingers as you wait for a quick resolution to the challenges of everyday living, take a deep breath and ask God for patience. Remember that patience builds character, and the best moment to start building is the present one.

More Thoughts about Patience

You can't step in front of God and not get in trouble. When He says, "Go three steps," don't go four.
CHARLES STANLEY

By His wisdom, He orders His delays so that they prove to be far better than our hurries.
C. H. SPURGEON

Patience is the companion of wisdom.
ST. AUGUSTINE

As we wait on God, He helps us use the winds of adversity to soar above our problems. As the Bible says, "Those who wait on the LORD . . . shall mount up with wings like eagles."
BILLY GRAHAM

Frustration is not the will of God. There is time to do anything and everything that God wants us to do.
ELISABETH ELLIOT

More from God's Word

A person's wisdom yields patience;
it is to one's glory to overlook an offense.
PROVERBS 19:11 NIV

Patience of spirit is better than haughtiness of spirit.
ECCLESIASTES 7:8 NASB

Better to be patient than powerful;
better to have self-control than to conquer a city.
PROVERBS 16:32 NLT

But if we hope for what we do not yet have,
we wait for it patiently.
ROMANS 8:25 NIV

Be joyful in hope, patient in affliction, faithful in prayer.
ROMANS 12:12 NIV

Remember This

The best things in life seldom happen overnight. Henry Blackaby wrote, "The grass that is here today and gone tomorrow does not require much time to mature. A big oak tree that lasts for generations requires much more time to grow and mature. God is concerned about your life through eternity. Allow Him to take all the time He needs to shape you for His purposes. Larger assignments will require longer periods of preparation." How true.

37

THE PROMISE: YOU CAN PARTAKE IN CHRIST'S JOY

I have spoken these things to you
so that My joy may be in you
and your joy may be complete.
JOHN 15:11 HCSB

Have you made the choice to rejoice, no matter your circumstances? Hopefully so. After all, if your life has been transformed by a personal relationship with God's only begotten Son, you have plenty of reasons to be joyful. Yet sometimes, when you're feeling discouraged or stressed, you may lose sight of your blessings as you wrestle with the challenges of everyday life.

Psalm 100 reminds us that, as believers, we have every reason to celebrate: "Shout for joy to the LORD, all the earth. Worship the LORD with gladness" (vv. 1–2 NIV). Are you worshipping the Lord with gladness? Hopefully so. But if you find yourself feeling discouraged or worse, it's time to slow down and have a quiet conversation with your Creator. If your heart is heavy, open the door of your soul to the Father and to His only begotten Son. Christ offers you His peace

and His joy. Accept it and share it freely, just as Christ has freely
shared His joy with you.

More Thoughts about Joy

Joy is the great note all throughout the Bible.
Oswald Chambers

Joy comes not from what we have but what we are.
C. H. Spurgeon

*As believers, our joy and peace are not based
in doing and achieving, but in believing.
Joy and peace come as a result of building
our relationship with the Lord.*
Joyce Meyer

*Joy is the settled assurance that God
is in control of all the details of my life,
the quiet confidence that ultimately
everything is going to be all right,
and the determined choice to praise God in all things.*
Kay Warren

Joy is the serious business of heaven.
C. S. Lewis

More from God's Word

*This is the day which the L*ORD *has made;*
let us rejoice and be glad in it.
PSALM 118:24 NASB

Rejoice in the Lord always.
Again I will say, rejoice!
PHILIPPIANS 4:4 NKJV

Rejoice always, pray without ceasing,
in everything give thanks;
for this is the will of God in Christ Jesus for you.
1 THESSALONIANS 5:16–18 NKJV

Until now you have asked for nothing
in My name. Ask and you will receive,
that your joy may be complete.
JOHN 16:24 HCSB

So you also have sorrow now. But I will see you again.
Your hearts will rejoice, and no one will rob you of your joy.
JOHN 16:22 HCSB

Remember This

Joy does not depend upon your circumstances; it depends upon your thoughts and upon your relationship with God.

38

THE PROMISE:
WHEN YOU'RE AN
ENTHUSIASTIC BELIEVER,
YOU'LL ACCOMPLISH MORE

Whatever you do, do it enthusiastically,
as something done for the Lord and not for men.
COLOSSIANS 3:23 HCSB

Are you passionate about your faith, your life, your family, and your future? Hopefully so. But if your zest for life has waned because of difficult circumstances, it is now time to redirect your efforts and recharge your spiritual batteries. And that means refocusing your priorities by putting God first.

Each day is a glorious opportunity to serve God and to do His will. Are you enthused about life, or do you struggle through each day giving scarcely a thought to God's blessings? Are you constantly praising God for His gifts, and are you sharing His Good News with the world? And are you excited about the possibilities for service that God has placed before you, whether at home, at work, or at church? You should be.

Norman Vincent Peale advised, "Get absolutely enthralled with something. Throw yourself into it with abandon. Get out of yourself. Be somebody. Do something." His words apply to you. So don't settle for a lukewarm existence. Instead, become genuinely involved—and fully engaged—in life. The world needs your enthusiasm . . . and so do you.

MORE THOUGHTS ABOUT ENTHUSIASM

We act as though comfort and luxury were the chief requirements of life, when all that we need to make us really happy is something to be enthusiastic about.
CHARLES KINGSLEY

Wherever you are, be all there. Live to the hilt every situation you believe to be the will of God.
JIM ELLIOT

Those who have achieved excellence in the practice of an art or profession have commonly been motivated by great enthusiasm in their pursuit of it.
JOHN KNOX

One of the great needs in the church today is for every Christian to become enthusiastic about his faith in Jesus Christ.
BILLY GRAHAM

It is a remarkable thing that some of the most optimistic and enthusiastic people you will meet are those who have been through intense suffering.
WARREN WIERSBE

More from God's Word

Do your work with enthusiasm.
Work as if you were serving the Lord,
not as if you were serving only men and women.
Ephesians 6:7 NCV

A happy heart makes the face cheerful,
but heartache crushes the spirit.
Proverbs 15:13 NIV

But as for me, I will hope continually,
and will praise You yet more and more.
Psalm 71:14 NASB

Rejoice always! Pray constantly.
Give thanks in everything,
for this is God's will for you in Christ Jesus.
1 Thessalonians 5:16–18 HCSB

Let the hearts of those who seek the Lord rejoice.
Look to the Lord and his strength; seek his face always.
1 Chronicles 16:10–11 NIV

A Timely Tip

Don't wait for enthusiasm to find you; make it your job to find it. Look at your life and your relationships as exciting adventures. Don't wait for life to spice itself; spice things up yourself.

39

The Promise: God's Truth Will Set You Free

You will know the truth, and the truth will set you free.
JOHN 8:32 HCSB

Would you like a rock-solid, time-tested formula for surviving difficult times? Here it is: seek God's truth, and live by it. Of course this strategy may sound simple, and it may sound somewhat old-fashioned. But God's truth never goes out of style, and God's wisdom is as valid today as it was when He laid the foundations of the universe.

The familiar words of John 8:32 remind us that the truth will set us free. And St. Augustine had this advice: "Let everything perish! Dismiss these empty vanities! And let us take up the search for the truth."

God is vitally concerned with truth. His Word teaches the truth; His Spirit reveals the truth; His Son leads us to the truth. When we open our hearts to the Lord, and when we allow His Son to rule over our thoughts and our lives, God reveals Himself, and we come to understand the truth about ourselves and the Truth (with a capital T) about God's gift of grace.

Are you seeking God's truth and making decisions in light of that truth? Hopefully so. When you do, you'll discover that the truth will indeed set you free, now and forever.

More Thoughts about Learning God's Truth

We have in Jesus Christ a perfect example of how to put God's truth into practice.
BILL BRIGHT

Those who walk in truth walk in liberty.
BETH MOORE

We learn His truth by obeying it.
OSWALD CHAMBERS

Truth will triumph. The Father of truth will win, and the followers of truth will be saved.
MAX LUCADO

Learning God's truth and getting it into our heads is one thing, but living God's truth and getting it into our characters is quite something else.
WARREN WIERSBE

More from God's Word

When the Spirit of truth comes,
He will guide you into all the truth.
John 16:13 HCSB

Jesus said, "I am the Road,
also the Truth, also the Life.
No one gets to the Father apart from me."
John 14:6 MSG

But do not follow foolish stories
that disagree with God's truth,
but train yourself to serve God.
1 Timothy 4:7 NCV

Learn the truth and never reject it.
Get wisdom, self-control, and understanding.
Proverbs 23:23 NCV

Teach me Your way, O Lord;
I will walk in Your truth.
Psalm 86:11 NASB

Remember This

Jesus offers you the Truth with a Capital T. How you respond to His Truth will determine the direction—and the destination—of your life.

40

THE PROMISE: THE LORD WILL HELP YOU MEET ANY CHALLENGE

So we may boldly say: "The LORD is my helper;
I will not fear. What can man do to me?"
HEBREWS 13:6 NKJV

Are you a confident believer, or do you live under a cloud of uncertainty and doubt? As a Christian, you have many reasons to be confident. After all, God is in His heaven; Christ has risen; and you are the recipient of God's grace. Despite these blessings, you may from time to time find yourself being tormented by negative emotions, and you are certainly not alone. Even the most faithful Christians are overcome by occasional bouts of fear and doubt.

Every life—including yours—is a series of successes and failures, celebrations and disappointments, joys and sorrows, hopes and fears. But even when you feel very distant from God, remember that God is never distant from you. When you sincerely seek His presence, He will touch your heart, calm your fears, and restore your confidence.

Doubts come in several shapes and sizes: doubts about God, doubts about the future, and doubts about your own abilities, for starters. And what, precisely, does God's Word say in response to these doubts? The Bible is clear: when you are beset by doubts, of whatever kind, you must draw closer to God through worship and through prayer (James 4:8).

The Lord promises that He will never leave your side, not for an instant. He is always with you, always willing to calm the storms of life. When you sincerely seek His presence—and when you genuinely seek to establish a deeper, more meaningful relationship with His Son—the Lord is prepared to touch your heart, to calm your fears, to answer your doubts, and to restore your confidence.

More Thoughts about Confidence

You need to make the right decision—
firmly and decisively—and then stick with it, with God's help.
BILLY GRAHAM

Never yield to gloomy anticipation.
LETTIE COWMAN

Confidence in the natural world is self-reliance;
in the spiritual world, it is God-reliance.
OSWALD CHAMBERS

We never get anywhere—nor do our conditions
and circumstances change—
when we look at the dark side of life.
LETTIE COWMAN

You cannot have a positive life and a negative mind.
JOYCE MEYER

More from God's Word

You are my hope; O Lord GOD, You are my confidence.
PSALM 71:5 NASB

*I lift up my eyes to the mountains—
where does my help come from? My help
comes from the LORD, the Maker of heaven and earth.*
PSALM 121:1–2 NIV

*God is our refuge and strength,
a very present help in trouble.*
PSALM 46:1 NKJV

*Be strong and courageous, and do the work.
Don't be afraid or discouraged, for the LORD God,
my God, is with you. He won't leave you or forsake you.*
1 CHRONICLES 28:20 HCSB

*In this world you will have trouble.
But take heart! I have overcome the world.*
JOHN 16:33 NIV

Remember This

Confidence in yourself is fine, but what you need most of all is confidence in God.

41

THE PROMISE: RIGHTEOUSNESS LEADS TO JOY AND PEACE

You will teach me how to live a holy life.
Being with you will fill me with joy;
at your right hand I will find pleasure forever.
PSALM 16:11 NCV

The Bible promises that the Lord will teach us how to live wisely and well. And one of the tools He uses to instruct us is His holy Word. God's Word is the ultimate guidebook for life here on earth and for life beyond the grave. The Bible is, therefore, a treasure beyond measure, and we must treat it that way.

This day, like every other, is filled to the brim with opportunities, challenges, and choices. But no choice that you make is more important than the choice you make concerning your heavenly Father. Today, you will either place Him at the center of your life—or not—and the consequences of that choice have implications that are both temporal and eternal.

Sometimes we don't intentionally neglect God; we simply allow ourselves to become overwhelmed with the demands of everyday life.

And then, without our even realizing it, we gradually drift away from the One we need most. Thankfully, God never drifts away from us. He remains always present, always steadfast, always loving.

So as you make the journey through and beyond difficult times, be sure to place God and His Son where they belong: in your head, in your prayers, on your lips, and in your heart. And then, with the Lord as your guide and companion, let the joyful journey begin.

MORE THOUGHTS ABOUT LIFE

The measure of a life, after all,
is not its duration but its donation.
CORRIE TEN BOOM

Wherever you are, be all there.
Live to the hilt every situation
you believe to be the will of God.
JIM ELLIOT

You have life before you. Only you can live it.
HENRY DRUMMOND

You can't control the length of your life—
but you can control its width and depth.
JOHN MAXWELL

Live out your life in its full meaning; it is God's life.
JOSIAH ROYCE

More from God's Word

I urge you to live a life worthy of the calling you have received.
EPHESIANS 4:1 NIV

*Jesus said to her, "I am the resurrection and the life.
The one who believes in Me, even if he dies, will live.
Everyone who lives and believes in Me
will never die—ever. Do you believe this?"*
JOHN 11:25–26 HCSB

*And Jesus said unto them, I am the bread of life:
he that cometh to me shall never hunger;
and he that believeth on me shall never thirst.*
JOHN 6:35 KJV

*He who follows righteousness and mercy finds life,
righteousness and honor.*
PROVERBS 21:21 NKJV

*Whoever finds their life will lose it,
and whoever loses their life for my sake will find it.*
MATTHEW 10:39 NIV

Remember This

Your life is a priceless opportunity, a gift of incalculable worth. Be thankful to the Giver and use His gift wisely while there's still time because night is coming when no one can work.

42

THE PROMISE: GOD CAN HELP YOU OVERCOME DISTRACTIONS AND FOCUS ON WHAT REALLY MATTERS

Let us lay aside every weight and the sin that so easily ensnares us. Let us run with endurance the race that lies before us, keeping our eyes on Jesus, the source and perfecter of our faith.
HEBREWS 12:1–2 HCSB

All of us must deal with an ever-increasing flood of interruptions and distractions. But when we find ourselves distracted by the minor frustrations of life, we must catch ourselves, take a deep breath, and lift our thoughts upward.

Although we must sometimes struggle mightily to rise above the distractions of everyday living, we need never struggle alone. God is here—eternal and faithful, with infinite patience and love—and if we reach out to Him, He will restore our sense of perspective.

Today, as you deal with difficult circumstances or unwelcome changes, make this promise to yourself and keep it: promise to focus your thoughts on things that are *really* important, things like your faith, your family, your friends, and your future. Don't allow the day's interruptions to derail your most important work. And don't allow other people (or, for that matter, the media) to decide what's important to you. Distractions are everywhere, but, thankfully, so is God . . . and that fact has everything to do with how you prioritize your day and live your life.

MORE THOUGHTS ABOUT DEALING WITH DISTRACTIONS

Setting goals is one way you can be sure that you will focus your efforts on the main things so that trivial matters will not become your focus.
CHARLES STANLEY

When Jesus is in our midst, He brings His limitless power along as well. But, Jesus must be in the middle, all eyes and hearts focused on Him.
SHIRLEY DOBSON

Among the enemies to devotion, none is so harmful as distractions. Whatever excites the curiosity, scatters the thoughts, disquiets the heart, absorbs the interests, or shifts our life focus from the kingdom of God within us to the world around us—that is a distraction; and the world is full of them.
A. W. TOZER

There is an enormous power in little things to distract our attention from God.
OSWALD CHAMBERS

More from God's Word

*But seek first the kingdom of God and His righteousness,
and all these things will be provided for you.*
MATTHEW 6:33 HCSB

*Patient endurance is what you need now,
so you will continue to do God's will.
Then you will receive all that he has promised.*
HEBREWS 10:36 NLT

*Trust in the LORD with all your heart, and do not rely
on your own understanding; think about Him
in all your ways, and He will guide you on the right paths.*
PROVERBS 3:5–6 HCSB

Let your eyes look forward; fix your gaze straight ahead.
PROVERBS 4:25 HCSB

*One thing I do, forgetting those things which
are behind and reaching forward to those things
which are ahead, I press toward the goal for the prize
of the upward call of God in Christ Jesus.*
PHILIPPIANS 3:13–14 NKJV

A Timely Tip

Take a few minutes to consider the everyday distractions that are
interfering with your life and your faith. Then jot down at least three
ideas for minimizing those distractions or eliminating them altogether.

43

THE PROMISE: THE LORD IS SUFFICIENT TO MEET EVERY NEED

My grace is sufficient for you,
for my power is made perfect in weakness.
2 CORINTHIANS 12:9 NIV

Do the demands of life seem overwhelming at times? If so, you must learn to rely not only upon your own resources, but also upon the promises of your Father in heaven. God will guide you and your family if you let Him. So even if your circumstances are difficult—even if your problems seem overwhelming—you must trust your heavenly Father.

The psalmist wrote, "Weeping may endure for a night, but joy comes in the morning" (Psalm 30:5 NKJV). But when we are suffering, the morning may seem very far away. It is not. God promises that He is "near to those who have a broken heart" (Psalm 34:18 NKJV). When we are troubled, we must turn to Him, and we must encourage our friends and family members to do likewise.

If you are discouraged by tough times or difficult circumstances, be mindful of this fact: The loving heart of God is sufficient to meet any challenge, including yours. In good times and hard times, the Lord is always sufficient to meet your needs. Always.

More Thoughts about God's Sufficiency

Jesus has been consistently affectionate and true to us.
He has shared His great wealth with us. How can we
doubt the all-powerful, all-sufficient Lord?
C. H. Spurgeon

God's saints in all ages have realized that
God was enough for them. God is enough for time;
God is enough for eternity. God is enough!
Hannah Whitall Smith

God is sufficient for all our needs, for every problem, for every
difficulty, for every broken heart, for every human sorrow.
Peter Marshall

The promises of God's Word sustain us
in our suffering, and we know Jesus sympathizes
and empathizes with us in our darkest hour.
Bill Bright

God is trying to get a message through to you,
and the message is: "Stop depending on inadequate
human resources. Let me handle the matter."
Catherine Marshall

More from God's Word

*And my God will supply all your needs according
to His riches in glory in Christ Jesus.*
PHILIPPIANS 4:19 HCSB

*For the eyes of the LORD are on the righteous,
and His ears are open to their prayers;
but the face of the LORD is against those who do evil.*
1 PETER 3:12 NKJV

*And God is able to make every grace overflow to you,
so that in every way, always having everything you need,
you may excel in every good work.*
2 CORINTHIANS 9:8 HCSB

*The LORD is my strength and song, and He has become
my salvation; He is my God, and I will praise Him.*
EXODUS 15:2 NKJV

*Take up My yoke and learn from Me, because I am gentle
and humble in heart, and you will find rest for yourselves.
For My yoke is easy and My burden is light.*
MATTHEW 11:29–30 HCSB

Remember This

If you'd like infinite protection, there's only one place you can
find it: from an infinite God. So remember: when you live in the
center of God's will, you will also be living in the center of God's
protection.

44

THE PROMISE: WHEN YOU GIVE GENEROUSLY, YOU WILL BE BLESSED

But this I say: He who sows sparingly will also reap sparingly, and he who sows bountifully will also reap bountifully. So let each one give as he purposes in his heart, not grudgingly or of necessity; for God loves a cheerful giver.

2 CORINTHIANS 9:6–7 NKJV

Every time you give generously to those who need your help, you're obeying the clear instructions of your Father in heaven. So if you're looking for a surefire way to improve the quality of your life, here it is: be more generous.

The thread of generosity is woven—completely and inextricably—into the very fabric of Christ's teachings. As He sent His disciples out to heal the sick and spread God's message of salvation, Jesus offered this guiding principle: "Freely you have received; freely give" (Matthew 10:8 NIV). The principle still applies. If we are to be disciples of Christ, we must give freely of our time, our possessions, and our love.

In 2 Corinthians 9, Paul reminds us that when we sow the seeds of generosity, we reap bountiful rewards in accordance with God's plan for our lives. Thus, we are instructed to give cheerfully and without reservation. So today and every day, give generously to those who are less fortunate than you. Find a need and fill it. Lend a helping hand and share a word of kindness. It's the right thing to do, and it's the best way to live.

More Thoughts about Generosity

Nothing is really ours until we share it.
C. S. Lewis

*The goodness you receive from God
is a treasure for you to share with others.*
Elizabeth George

We are never more like God than when we give.
Charles Swindoll

Generosity is changing one's focus from self to others.
John Maxwell

*God does not supply money to satisfy
our every whim and desire. His promise
is to meet our needs and provide an abundance
so that we can help other people.*
Larry Burkett

More from God's Word

Freely you have received; freely give.
MATTHEW 10:8 NIV

You should remember the words of the Lord Jesus:
"It is more blessed to give than to receive."
ACTS 20:35 NLT

If you have two shirts, give one to the poor.
If you have food, share it with those who are hungry.
LUKE 3:11 NLT

Whenever we have the opportunity, we should do good
to everyone—especially to those in the family of faith.
GALATIANS 6:10 NLT

Truly I tell you, whatever you did for one of the least of these
brothers and sisters of mine, you did for me.
MATTHEW 25:40 NIV

A Timely Tip

Would you like to be a little happier? Try sharing a few more of the blessings that God has bestowed upon you. In other words, if you want to be happy, be generous. And if you want to be unhappy, be greedy. And if you're not sure about the best way to give, pray about it.

45

THE PROMISE: THE LORD WILL PROTECT YOU

The LORD is my shepherd, I shall not want.
He makes me lie down in green pastures; He leads
me beside quiet waters. He restores my soul.
PSALM 23:1–3 NASB

Time and again, the Bible promises that the Lord will protect those of us who honor and obey Him. But because we are imperfect human beings living imperfect lives, we worry. Even though we, as Christians, have the assurance of eternal life—even though we, as believers, have the promise of God's love and protection—we find ourselves fretting over the countless details of everyday life. Jesus understood our concerns, and He addressed them.

In Matthew, Jesus makes it clear that God is, indeed, our Shepherd:

> Therefore I say to you, do not worry about your life, what you will eat or what you will drink; nor about your body, what you will put on. Is not life more than food and the body more than clothing? Look at the birds of

the air, for they neither sow nor reap nor gather into barns; yet your heavenly Father feeds them. Are you not of more value than they? Which of you by worrying can add one cubit to his stature? . . . Therefore do not worry about tomorrow, for tomorrow will worry about its own things. Sufficient for the day is its own trouble (6:25–27, 34 NKJV).

Perhaps you are uncertain about your future, your finances, your relationships, or your health. Or perhaps you are simply a "worrier" by nature. If so, make Matthew 6 a regular part of your daily Bible reading. This beautiful passage will remind you that God still sits in His heaven, and you are His beloved child. Then, perhaps, you will worry a little less and trust God a little more, and that's as it should be because God is trustworthy, and you are protected.

MORE THOUGHTS ABOUT GOD'S PROTECTION

A mighty fortress is our God,
a bulwark never failing;
our helper He, amid the flood
of mortal ills prevailing.
MARTIN LUTHER

Only believe, don't fear. Our Master, Jesus,
always watches over us, and no matter what
the persecution, Jesus will surely overcome it.
LOTTIE MOON

The safest place in all the world
is in the will of God, and the safest protection
in all the world is the name of God.

As you walk through the valley of the unknown,
you will find the footprints of Jesus
both in front of you and beside you.

CHARLES STANLEY

Measure the size of the obstacles
against the size of God.

BETH MOORE

More from God's Word

The LORD is my light and my salvation—
whom should I fear? The LORD is the stronghold of my life—
of whom should I be afraid?

PSALM 27:1 HCSB

As for God, His way is perfect;
the word of the LORD is proven;
He is a shield to all who trust in Him.

PSALM 18:30 NKJV

The LORD is my rock, my fortress,
and my deliverer, my God,
my mountain where I seek refuge.
My shield, the horn of my salvation,
my stronghold, my refuge, and my Savior.
2 SAMUEL 22:2–3 HCSB

Those who trust in the LORD are like Mount Zion.
It cannot be shaken; it remains forever.
PSALM 125:1 HCSB

So we may boldly say:
"The LORD is my helper; I will not fear.
What can man do to me?"
HEBREWS 13:6 NKJV

Remember This

When it comes to solving problems, work beats worry and trust beats anxiety. So instead of fretting about your troubles, get busy tackling the problems that you can solve, and turn everything else over to the Lord.

46

THE PROMISE:
IF YOU ACKNOWLEDGE
YOUR SHORTCOMINGS,
YOU WILL BE FORGIVEN

*If we confess our sins, He is faithful and righteous to forgive
us our sins and to cleanse us from all unrighteousness.*
1 JOHN 1:9 NASB

The Bible promises us that the Lord will forgive our sins if we ask
Him for forgiveness. It's our duty to ask, and when we've fulfilled
that responsibility, He will always fulfill His promise. Yet many of us
continue to punish ourselves—with needless guilt and self-loathing—
for mistakes that our Creator has long since forgiven and forgotten
(Isaiah 43:25).

If you haven't managed to forgive yourself for some past mistake
or for a series of poor decisions, it's time to rearrange your thinking.
If God has forgiven you, how can you withhold forgiveness from
yourself? The answer, of course, is that God's mercy is intended to
wash your sins away. That's what the Lord wants, and if you're good
enough for Him, you're good enough.

More Thoughts about God's Forgiveness

*God's mercy is boundless, free,
and, through Jesus Christ our Lord,
available to us in our present situation.*
A. W. Tozier

*Forgiveness is an opportunity that God
extended to us on the cross. When we accept
His forgiveness and are willing
to forgive ourselves, then we find relief.*
Billy Graham

We cannot out-sin God's ability to forgive us.
Beth Moore

*The most marvelous ingredient in the forgiveness
of God is that He also forgets, the one thing
a human being cannot do. With God, forgetting
is a divine attribute. God's forgiveness forgets.*
Oswald Chambers

*God does not wish us to remember
what He is willing to forget.*
George A. Buttrick

More from God's Word

All the prophets testify about Him that through
His name everyone who believes in
Him will receive forgiveness of sins.
ACTS 10:43 HCSB

Let us, then, feel very sure that we can come
before God's throne where there is grace.
There we can receive mercy and grace
to help us when we need it.
HEBREWS 4:16 NCV

But the mercy of the LORD is from everlasting
to everlasting upon them that fear him,
and his righteousness unto children's children.
PSALM 103:17 KJV

Be merciful, just as your Father is merciful.
LUKE 6:36 NIV

It is I who sweep away your transgressions
for My own sake and remember your sins no more.
ISAIAH 43:25 HCSB

Remember This

You cannot do anything that God can't forgive. God forgives sin when you ask, so ask. God stands ready to forgive. The next move is yours.

47

THE PROMISE: TRUE GREATNESS IS ACHIEVED THROUGH SERVICE

He who is greatest among you shall be your servant.
And whoever exalts himself will be humbled,
and he who humbles himself will be exalted.

MATTHEW 23:11–12 NKJV

We live in a world that glorifies power, prestige, fame, and money. But the words of Jesus teach us that the most esteemed men and women in this world are not the self-congratulatory leaders of society but are instead the humblest of servants. So if you genuinely seek to discover God's unfolding purpose for your life, you must ask yourself this question: how does the Lord want me to serve?

Whatever your path, whatever your calling, you may be certain of this: Service to others is an integral part of God's plan for you. Christ was the ultimate servant, the Savior who gave His life for mankind. If we are to follow Him, we, too, must become humble servants.

Every day of your life, including this one, God will give you opportunities to serve Him by serving His children. Welcome those opportunities with open arms. They are God's gift to you, His way of allowing you to achieve greatness in His kingdom.

More Thoughts about Service

Our voices, our service, and our abilities are to be employed, primarily, for the glory of God.
Billy Graham

Your attitude of serving the Lord can transform even the most menial of tasks into a magnificent sacrifice of love.
Elizabeth George

Faithful servants never retire. You can retire from your career, but you will never retire from serving God.
Rick Warren

Have thy tools ready; God will find thee work.
Charles Kingsley

In the very place where God has put us, whatever its limitations, whatever kind of work it may be, we may indeed serve the Lord Christ.
Elisabeth Elliot

More from God's Word

Shepherd God's flock, for whom you are responsible.
Watch over them because you want to,
not because you are forced. That is how God wants it.
Do it because you are happy to serve.
1 PETER 5:2 NCV

As each one has received a gift, minister it to one another,
as good stewards of the manifold grace of God.
1 PETER 4:10 NKJV

Blessed are those servants, whom the lord
when he cometh shall find watching.
LUKE 12:37 KJV

Assuredly, I say to you, inasmuch as you
did it to one of the least of these
My brethren, you did it to Me.
MATTHEW 25:40 NKJV

Even so faith, if it hath not works,
is dead, being alone.
JAMES 2:17 KJV

Remember This

God wants you to serve Him now, not later. So don't put off until tomorrow the good works you can perform for Him today.

48

THE PROMISE: WE ARE ALL ACCOUNTABLE FOR THE WORDS WE SPEAK

I tell you that on the day of judgment people
will have to account for every careless word
they speak. For by your words you will be acquitted,
and by your words you will be condemned.

MATTHEW 12:36–37 HCSB

Time and again, God's Word teaches us that we are personally responsible for the words we speak. And the Bible warns us against angry outbursts and needless arguments. Arguments are seldom won but often lost, so when we acquire the unfortunate habit of habitual bickering, we do harm to our friends, to our families, to our coworkers, and to ourselves. And when we engage in petty squabbles, our losses usually outpace our gains.

Most arguments are a monumental waste of time and energy. And most squabbles do more for the devil than they do for the Lord. So the next time you're tempted to engage in a silly squabble, slow down, catch your breath, and hold your tongue.

You have the power to lift your friends, your family members, and your coworkers. But you also have the power to hold them back or put them down. When you learn how to lift them up, truthfully and compassionately, you'll soon discover that you've lifted yourself up too.

More Thoughts about Avoiding Needless Arguments

We must meet our disappointments, our malicious enemies,
our provoking friends, our trials of every sort,
with an attitude of surrender and trust. We must rise
above them in Christ so they lose their power to harm us.
Hannah Whitall Smith

Forgiveness is the economy of the heart.
Forgiveness saves the expense of anger,
the cost of hatred, the waste of spirits.
Hannah More

Grudges are like hand grenades: it is wise
to release them before they destroy you.
Barbara Johnson

Hot heads and cold hearts never solved anything.
Billy Graham

Never persist in trying to set people right.
Hannah Whitall Smith

More from God's Word

Do everything without grumbling and arguing,
so that you may be blameless and pure.
PHILIPPIANS 2:14–15 HCSB

If any man among you seem to be religious,
and bridleth not his tongue, but deceiveth
his own heart, this man's religion is vain.
JAMES 1:26 KJV

A soft answer turneth away wrath:
but grievous words stir up anger.
PROVERBS 15:1 KJV

People with quick tempers cause trouble,
but those who control their tempers stop a quarrel.
PROVERBS 15:18 NCV

Avoiding a fight is a mark of honor;
only fools insist on quarreling.
PROVERBS 20:3 NLT

A Timely Tip

Arguments usually cause many more problems than they solve. So don't be afraid to leave the scene of an argument.

49

THE PROMISE: THE LORD WILL GIVE YOU STRENGTH TO RESIST THE ENEMY

Be sober, be vigilant; because your adversary the devil walks about like a roaring lion, seeking whom he may devour.

1 PETER 5:8 NKJV

This world is God's creation, and it contains the wonderful fruits of His handiwork. But the world also contains countless opportunities to stray from God's will. Temptations are everywhere, and the devil never takes a day off. Our task, as believers, is to turn away from temptation and to place our lives squarely in the center of God's will.

Evil is indeed abroad in the world, and Satan continues to sow the seeds of destruction far and wide. In a very real sense, our world is at war: good versus evil, sin versus righteousness, hope versus suffering, praise versus apathy. As Christians, we must ensure that we place ourselves squarely on the right side of these conflicts: God's side. How can we do it? By thoughtfully studying God's Word, by regularly worshiping with fellow believers, and by guarding our hearts and minds against the subtle temptations of the enemy. When we do, we are protected.

Are you determined to stand up against evil whenever and wherever you confront it? And are you fully prepared to distance yourself from the countless temptations that have become so thoroughly woven into the fabric of society? If so, congratulations. That means you're an active-duty participant in the battle against a powerful and dangerous adversary. And with God's help, you're destined to win the battle *and* the war.

More Thoughts about Evil

Measure your growth in grace by your sensitivity to sin.
Oswald Chambers

*Just as courage is faith in good, so discouragement
is faith in evil, and, while courage opens
the door to good, discouragement opens it to evil.*
Hannah Whitall Smith

*Self is the root, the branches, the tree,
of all the evil of our fallen state.*
Andrew Murray

*Evil is present, often cleverly disguised as good.
Evil is present to control and deceive us.*
Billy Graham

Evil is real—but so is God's power and love.
Billy Graham

More from God's Word

*Put on the full armor of God so that you
can stand against the tactics of the Devil.*
EPHESIANS 6:11 HCSB

*Therefore submit to God. Resist the devil and he will
flee from you. Draw near to God and He will draw
near to you. Cleanse your hands, you sinners;
and purify your hearts, you double-minded.*
JAMES 4:7–8 NKJV

*Don't fear those who kill the body but
are not able to kill the soul; but rather, fear Him
who is able to destroy both soul and body in hell.*
MATTHEW 10:28 HCSB

*Dear friend, do not imitate what is evil,
but what is good. The one who does good is of God;
the one who does evil has not seen God.*
3 JOHN 1:11 HCSB

*The house of the wicked shall be overthrown:
but the tabernacle of the upright shall flourish.*
PROVERBS 14:11 KJV

Remember This

Evil exists, and it exists someplace not too far from you. You must
guard your steps and your heart accordingly.

50

THE PROMISE:
GOD HAS GIVEN YOU
TALENTS, AND HE WANTS
YOU TO USE THEM

I remind you to keep ablaze the gift of God that is in you.
2 TIMOTHY 1:6 HCSB

All of us have special talents, and you are no exception. But your talent is no guarantee of success; it must be cultivated and nurtured. Otherwise, it will go unused, and God's gift to you will be squandered.

In Matthew 25, Jesus tells the parable of the talents. In it, He describes a master who leaves his servants with varying amounts of money (talents). When the master returns, some servants have put their money to work and earned more, to which the master responds, "Well done, good and faithful servant! You have been faithful with a few things; I will put you in charge of many things. Come and share your master's happiness!" (vv. 21, 23 NIV).

But the story does not end so happily for the foolish servant who was given a single talent but did nothing with it. For this man, the master has nothing but reproach: "You wicked, lazy servant!" (v. 26). The message from Jesus is clear: We must use our talents, not waste them.

Your particular talent is a treasure on temporary loan from the Creator. He intends that your talent enrich the world and enrich your life. Even when you're enduring difficult times, you must value the gift that God has given you. And you must share your talents with the world. Then when you meet your Master face-to-face, you, too, will hear those wonderful words, "Well done, good and faithful servant! . . . Come and share your Master's happiness!"

MORE THOUGHTS ABOUT USING YOUR TALENTS

You aren't an accident. You were deliberately planned, specifically gifted, and lovingly positioned on this earth by the Master Craftsman.
MAX LUCADO

You are the only person on earth who can use your ability.
ZIG ZIGLAR

Employ whatever God has entrusted you with, in doing good, all possible good, in every possible kind and degree.
JOHN WESLEY

If you want to reach your potential, you need to add a strong work ethic to your talent.
JOHN MAXWELL

If others don't use their gifts, you get cheated, and if you don't use your gifts, they get cheated.
RICK WARREN

More from God's Word

Do not neglect the gift that is in you.
1 Timothy 4:14 NKJV

*God has given each of you a gift from his great variety
of spiritual gifts. Use them well to serve one another.*
1 Peter 4:10 NLT

Now there are diversities of gifts, but the same Spirit.
1 Corinthians 12:4 KJV

*Every good and perfect gift is from above,
coming down from the Father of the heavenly lights,
who does not change like shifting shadows.*
James 1:17 NIV

*Do not be afraid or discouraged.
For the LORD your God is with you wherever you go.*
Joshua 1:9 NLT

Remember This

Converting raw talent into polished skill usually requires work, and lots of it. God's Word clearly instructs you to do the hard work of refining your talents for the glory of His kingdom and the service of His people. So we are wise to remember the old adage: "What you are is God's gift to you; what you become is your gift to God." And it's up to you to make sure that your gift is worthy of the Giver.

51

THE PROMISE: BECAUSE JESUS OFFERS PEACE, YOU NEED NOT BE AFRAID

Peace I leave with you; My peace I give to you;
not as the world gives do I give to you.
Do not let your heart be troubled, nor let it be fearful.
JOHN 14:27 NASB

We live in a world that can, at times, be a very frightening place. We live in a world that is, at times, a very discouraging place. We live in a world where life-changing losses can be so painful and so profound that it seems we will never recover. But with God's help and with the help of encouraging family members and friends, we *can* recover.

During the darker days of life, we are wise to remember the words of Jesus, who reassured His disciples, saying, "Take courage! It is I. Don't be afraid" (Matthew 14:27 NIV).

Are you willing to face your fears right now? Are you willing to cast off the chains of timidity and procrastination by deciding to do what needs to be done now, not "later"? If the answer to these questions is yes, then you're destined to build a better life for yourself and your loved ones.

Today, ask God for the courage to step beyond the boundaries of your self-doubts. Ask Him to guide you to a place where you can realize your full potential—a place where you are freed from the fear of failure. Ask Him to do His part, and promise Him that you will do your part. Don't ask Him to lead you to a "safe" place; ask Him to lead you to the "right" place . . . and remember: those two places are seldom the same.

More Thoughts about Fear

When we meditate on God and remember the promises He has given us in His Word, our faith grows, and our fears dissolve.
Charles Stanley

You needn't worry about not feeling brave.
Our Lord didn't—see the scene in Gethsemane.
How thankful I am that when God became man He did
not choose to become a man of iron nerves; that would
not have helped weaklings like you and me nearly so much.
C. S. Lewis

The presence of fear does not mean you have no faith. Fear visits everyone. But make your fear a visitor and not a resident.
Max Lucado

It is good to remind ourselves that the will of God comes from the heart of God and that we need not be afraid.
Warren Wiersbe

MORE FROM GOD'S WORD

But He said to them, "It is I; do not be afraid."
JOHN 6:20 NKJV

Fear not, for I am with you; be not dismayed,
for I am your God. I will strengthen you,
Yes, I will help you, I will uphold you
with My righteous right hand.
ISAIAH 41:10 NKJV

The LORD is my light and my salvation—
whom should I fear? The LORD is the
stronghold of my life—of whom should I be afraid?
PSALM 27:1 HCSB

Even though I walk through the darkest valley,
I will fear no evil, for you are with me;
your rod and your staff, they comfort me.
PSALM 23:4 NIV

Be not afraid, only believe.
MARK 5:36 KJV

A TIMELY TIP

Are you feeling anxious or fearful? If so, trust God to handle those problems that are simply too big for you to solve. Entrust the future—your future—to God. Then spend a few minutes thinking about specific steps you can take to confront—and conquer—your fears.

52

THE PROMISE: STRIVING TO PLEASE OTHER PEOPLE IS DANGEROUS

The fear of man is a snare,
but the one who trusts in the LORD is protected.
PROVERBS 29:25 HCSB

It feels good to be popular. That's why so many of us invest so much time, so much energy, and so much personal capital trying to gain the approval of our peers. But oftentimes, in our effort to gain earthly approval, we make spiritual sacrifices. Big mistake.

It always pays to put God first and keep Him there. When we do, our other priorities tend to fall into place. But when we focus too intently on worldly pursuits, we suffer.

As you make decisions throughout the day, it's wise to think less about pleasing people and more about pleasing your Creator. It's the best way—and the safest way—to live.

So who will you try to please today: God or man? Your primary obligation is not to imperfect men and women. Your obligation is to strive diligently to meet the expectations of an all-knowing and perfect God. Trust Him always. Love Him always. Praise Him always. And seek to please Him. Always.

More Thoughts about Pleasing God First

If pleasing people is your goal,
you will be enslaved to them.
People can be harsh taskmasters
when you give them this power over you.
SARAH YOUNG

Stop determining your worth and value
by what other people say. Be determined
by what the Word of God says.
JOYCE MEYER

The major problem with letting others define you
is that it borders on idolatry. Your concern to please
others dampens your desire to please your Creator.
SARAH YOUNG

Don't pay much attention to who is for you
and who is against you. This is your major concern:
that God be with you in everything you do.
THOMAS À KEMPIS

Anyone who tries to keep all the people happy
all the time will never fulfill their destiny.
JOYCE MEYER

MORE FROM GOD'S WORD

For am I now trying to win the favor of people, or God?
Or am I striving to please people? If I were still trying
to please people, I would not be a slave of Christ.
GALATIANS 1:10 HCSB

It is better to take refuge in the LORD than to trust in man.
PSALM 118:8 HCSB

My son, if sinners entice you, don't be persuaded.
PROVERBS 1:10 HCSB

Keep your eyes focused on what is right.
Keep looking straight ahead to what is good.
PROVERBS 4:25 ICB

Do not be unequally yoked together with unbelievers.
For what fellowship has righteousness with lawlessness?
And what communion has light with darkness?
2 CORINTHIANS 6:14 NKJV

REMEMBER THIS

Being obedient to God means that you can't always please other
people. Sometimes you've got to please God, no matter what anybody
else thinks or says.

53

THE PROMISE:
IF WE JUDGE OTHERS,
WE CONDEMN OURSELVES

Therefore, any one of you who judges is without excuse.
For when you judge another, you condemn yourself,
since you, the judge, do the same things.
ROMANS 2:1 HCSB

The need to judge others seems woven into the very fabric of human consciousness. We mortals feel compelled to serve as informal judges and juries, pronouncing our own verdicts on the actions and perceived motivations of others, all the while excusing—or oftentimes hiding—our own shortcomings. But God's Word instructs us to let Him be the judge. He knows that we, with our limited knowledge and personal biases, are simply ill-equipped to assess the actions of others. The act of judging, then, becomes not only an act of futility, but also an affront to our Creator.

When Jesus came upon a woman who had been condemned by the Pharisees, He spoke not only to the people who had gathered there, but also to all generations. Christ warned, "He that is without sin among you, let him first cast a stone at her" (John 8:7 KJV). The message is clear: because we are all sinners, we must refrain from the temptation to judge others.

So the next time you're tempted to cast judgment on another human being, resist that temptation. God hasn't called you to be a judge; He's called you to be a witness. And He wants you to be a worthy witness, not an unqualified judge.

MORE THOUGHTS ABOUT JUDGING OTHERS

We must learn to regard people less in the light
of what they do or omit to do,
and more in light of what they suffer.
DIETRICH BONHOEFFER

Don't judge other people more harshly
than you want God to judge you.
MARIE T. FREEMAN

Yes, let God be the Judge.
Your job today is to be a witness.
WARREN WIERSBE

Judging draws the judgment of others.
CATHERINE MARSHALL

Oh, how horrible our sins look when
they are committed by someone else.
CHARLES SWINDOLL

More from God's Word

Don't criticize one another, brothers. He who criticizes a brother or judges his brother criticizes the law and judges the law. But if you judge the law, you are not a doer of the law but a judge.
JAMES 4:11 HCSB

Judge not, and you shall not be judged. Condemn not, and you shall not be condemned. Forgive, and you will be forgiven.
LUKE 6:37 NKJV

Do everything without grumbling and arguing, so that you may be blameless and pure.
PHILIPPIANS 2:14–15 HCSB

Those who guard their lips preserve their lives, but those who speak rashly will come to ruin.
PROVERBS 13:3 NIV

Let the words of my mouth and the meditation of my heart be acceptable in Your sight, O LORD, my strength and my Redeemer.
PSALM 19:14 NKJV

A Timely Tip

If you catch yourself being overly judgmental, slow down long enough to interrupt those critical thoughts before they hijack your emotions and wreck your day.

54

THE PROMISE: BECAUSE THE LORD CARES FOR YOU, HE WILL SUPPORT YOU

Therefore humble yourselves under the mighty
hand of God, that He may exalt you in due time,
casting all your care upon Him, for He cares for you.
1 PETER 5:6–7 NKJV

God has promised to lift you up and guide your steps if you let Him. God has promised that when you entrust your life to Him completely and without reservation, He will give you the strength to meet any challenge, the courage to face any trial, and the wisdom to live in His righteousness.

The Lord promises to support and protect those who turn their hearts and prayers to Him. Will you count yourself among that number? Will you accept God's peace and wear God's armor against the temptations and distractions of our dangerous world? If you do, you can live courageously and optimistically, knowing that you are protected by your loving heavenly Father.

So today, as you encounter the inevitable challenges of everyday life, remember that the Lord never leaves you, not even for a moment. He's always available, always ready to listen, always ready to lead. When you make a habit of talking to Him early and often, He'll guide you and comfort you every day of your life.

MORE THOUGHTS ABOUT GOD'S SUPPORT

Put your hand into the hand of God.
He gives the calmness and serenity of heart and soul.
LETTIE COWMAN

The knowledge that we are never alone
calms the troubled sea of our lives
and speaks peace to our souls.
A. W. TOZER

The will of God is either a burden we carry
or a power which carries us.
CORRIE TEN BOOM

When once we are assured that God is good,
then there can be nothing left to fear.
HANNAH WHITALL SMITH

Measure the size of the obstacles against the size of God.
BETH MOORE

MORE FROM GOD'S WORD

Nevertheless God, who comforts the downcast, comforted us.
2 CORINTHIANS 7:6 NKJV

My grace is sufficient for you,
for my power is made perfect in weakness.
2 CORINTHIANS 12:9 NIV

Therefore, we may boldly say:
The Lord is my helper; I will not be afraid.
What can man do to me?
HEBREWS 13:6 HCSB

The LORD is my light and my salvation—
whom should I fear? The LORD is the
stronghold of my life—of whom should I be afraid?
PSALM 27:1 HCSB

The LORD is my shepherd; I shall not want.
He makes me to lie down in green pastures;
He leads me beside the still waters. He restores my soul.
PSALM 23:1–3 NKJV

A TIMELY TIP

Today, think about God's power to help you bring about miraculous changes in your life. And then, take a few moments to pray about the changes you'd like to make. And remember this: when you ask God for His help, He will provide it.

55

THE PROMISE: JESUS LOVES YOU

As the Father loved Me,
I also have loved you; abide in My love.
JOHN 15:9 NKJV

The Bible promises that Jesus loves us. So how much does He love us? More than we, as mere mortals, can comprehend. His love is perfect and steadfast. Even though we are fallible and wayward, the Good Shepherd cares for us still. Even though we have fallen far short of the Father's commandments, Christ loves us with a depth that is beyond our understanding. The sacrifice that Jesus made upon the cross was made for each of us, and His love endures to the edge of eternity and beyond.

Christ's love changes everything. When you accept His gift of grace, you are transformed, not only for today, but also for all eternity. If you haven't already done so, invite Him into your heart. He's waiting patiently for you to walk with Him now and forever. Please don't make Him wait a single minute longer.

MORE THOUGHTS ABOUT CHRIST'S LOVE

Jesus is all compassion.
He never betrays us.
CATHERINE MARSHALL

Jesus: the proof of God's love.
PHILLIP YANCEY

As the love of a husband for his bride,
such is the love of Christ for His people.
C. H. SPURGEON

The love of God exists in its strongest
and purest form in the very midst
of suffering and tragedy.
SUZANNE DALE EZELL

Above all else, the Christian life
is a love affair of the heart.
JOHN ELDREDGE

More from God's Word

*I am the good shepherd. The good shepherd
lays down his life for the sheep.*

JOHN 10:11 HCSB

*No one has greater love than this, that someone
would lay down his life for his friends.*

JOHN 15:13 HCSB

*For Christ also suffered once for sins,
the just for the unjust, that He might
bring us to God, being put to death
in the flesh but made alive by the Spirit.*

1 PETER 3:18 NKJV

We love him, because he first loved us.

1 JOHN 4:19 KJV

*For God so loved the world, that he gave
his only begotten Son, that whosoever believeth
in him should not perish, but have everlasting life.*

JOHN 3:16 KJV

Remember This

Christ's love is meant to be experienced—and shared—by you.

56

THE PROMISE: GOD DOESN'T HOLD OUR MISTAKES AGAINST US (AND NEITHER SHOULD WE)

If we confess our sins, He is faithful and righteous to forgive us our sins and to cleanse us from all unrighteousness.
1 JOHN 1:9 HCSB

Everybody makes mistakes, and so will you. In fact, Winston Churchill once observed, "Success is going from failure to failure without loss of enthusiasm." What was good for Churchill is also good for you. You should expect to make mistakes—plenty of them—but you should not allow those missteps to rob you of the enthusiasm you need to fulfill God's plan for your life.

We are imperfect people living in an imperfect world; mistakes are simply part of the price we pay for being here. But even though mistakes are an inevitable part of life's journey, repeated mistakes should not be. When we commit the inevitable blunders of life, we must correct them, learn from them, and pray for the wisdom not to repeat them. When we do, our mistakes become lessons, and our experiences become adventures in character building.

When our shortcomings are made public, we may feel embarrassed or worse. We may presume (quite incorrectly) that "everybody" is concerned with the gravity of our problem. And, as a consequence, we may feel the need to hide from our problems rather than confront them. To do so is wrong. Even when our pride is bruised, we must face up to our mistakes and seek to rise above them.

Have you made a king-sized blunder or two? Of course you have. But here's the big question: Have you used your mistakes as stumbling blocks or stepping stones? The answer to this question will determine how well you perform in the workplace and in every other aspect of your life. So don't let the fear of past failures hold you back. Instead, own up to your mistakes, do your best to fix them, and be sure to learn from them. And while you're at it, please remember this: even if you've make a colossal blunder, God isn't finished with you yet—in fact, He's probably just getting started.

More Thoughts about Learning from Mistakes

I hope you don't mind me telling you all this.
One can learn only by seeing one's mistakes.
C. S. Lewis

Truth will sooner come out of error than from confusion.
Francis Bacon

Lord, when we are wrong, make us willing to change;
and when we are right, make us easy to live with.
Peter Marshall

Father, take our mistakes and turn them into opportunities.
MAX LUCADO

MORE FROM GOD'S WORD

He who covers his sins will not prosper,
but whoever confesses and forsakes them will have mercy.
PROVERBS 28:13 NKJV

Therefore let us approach the throne of grace
with boldness, so that we may receive mercy
and find grace to help us at the proper time.
HEBREWS 4:16 HCSB

But the mercy of the LORD is from everlasting
to everlasting upon them that fear him,
and his righteousness unto children's children.
PSALM 103:17 KJV

Therefore, if anyone is in Christ,
he is a new creation; old things have passed away;
behold, all things have become new.
2 CORINTHIANS 5:17 NKJV

A TIMELY TIP

When you make a mistake, the time to make things better is now, not later. The sooner you address your problem, the better. If not now, when?

57

THE PROMISE: GOD'S WORD CAN LIGHT YOUR PATH

Your word is a lamp for my feet and a light on my path.
PSALM 119:105 HCSB

God's promises are found in a book like no other: the Holy Bible. The Bible is a roadmap for life here on earth and for life eternal. As Christians, we are called upon to trust its promises, to follow its commandments, and to share its Good News.

The Lord has made promises to mankind and to you. God's promises never fail and they never grow old. You must trust those promises and share them with your family, with your friends, and with the world.

Are you standing on the promises of God? Are you expecting Him to do wonderful things, or are you living beneath a cloud of apprehension and doubt? The familiar words of Psalm 118:24 remind us of a profound yet simple truth: "This is the day which the LORD hath made; we will rejoice and be glad in it" (KJV). Do you trust that promise, and do you live accordingly? If so, you are living the passionate life that God intends.

As we face the inevitable challenges and disappointments of life here on earth, we must arm ourselves with the promises of God's holy Word. When we do, we can expect the best, not only for the day ahead, but also for all eternity.

More Thoughts about God's Word

Reading news without reading the Bible
will inevitably lead to an unbalanced life,
an anxious spirit, a worried and depressed soul.
BILL BRIGHT

God gives us a compass and a Book of promises and principles—
the Bible—and lets us make our decisions day by day as we
sense the leading of His Spirit. This is how we grow.
WARREN WIERSBE

All the good from the Savior of the world is communicated
through this book; but for the book we could not know right
from wrong. All the things desirable to man are contained in it.
ABRAHAM LINCOLN

The Bible is God's Word, given to us by God Himself
so we can know Him and His will for our lives.
BILLY GRAHAM

Try to get saturated with the gospel.
C. H. SPURGEON

More from God's Word

*For the word of God is living and effective and sharper
than any double-edged sword, penetrating as far as the
separation of soul and spirit, joints and marrow.
It is able to judge the ideas and thoughts of the heart.*
Hebrews 4:12 HCSB

*Jesus answered, "It is written:
'Man does not live by bread alone,
but on every word that comes from the mouth of God.'"*
Matthew 4:4 NIV

*All scripture is given by inspiration of God,
and is profitable for doctrine, for reproof, for correction,
for instruction in righteousness.*
2 Timothy 3:16 KJV

*Therefore everyone who hears these words
of mine and puts them into practice is like
a wise man who built his house on the rock.*
Mathew 7:24 NIV

Remember This

Charles Swindoll wrote, "There are four words I wish we would never forget, and they are, 'God keeps His word.'" And remember: when it comes to studying God's Word, school is always in session.

58

THE PROMISE: WHEN YOU PRAISE THE LORD WITH A GRATEFUL HEART, YOU WILL BE BLESSED

Let everything that breathes praise the LORD. Hallelujah!
PSALM 150:6 HCSB

If you're in the midst of difficult times, perhaps you're feeling sorry for yourself. Or perhaps you're feeling discouraged or worried or worse. If so, here's a time-tested remedy for those negative feelings: try spending less time focusing on your disappointments and more time praising God.

So when is the best time to praise God? In church? Before dinner is served? When we tuck little children into bed? None of the above. The best time to praise God is all day, every day, to the greatest extent we can, with thanksgiving in our hearts.

Too many of us, even well-intentioned believers, tend to compartmentalize our waking hours into a few familiar categories: work, rest, play, family time, and worship. To do so is a mistake. Worship and praise should be woven into the fabric of everything we do; it should never be relegated to a weekly three-hour visit to church on Sunday morning.

Mrs. Charles E. Cowman, the author of the classic devotional text *Streams in the Desert*, wrote, "Two wings are necessary to lift our souls toward God: prayer and praise. Prayer asks. Praise accepts the answer." Today, find a little more time to lift your concerns to God in prayer, and praise Him for all that He has done. He's listening . . . and He wants to hear directly from you.

More Thoughts about Praise

Be not afraid of saying too much in the praises of God;
all the danger is of saying too little.
Matthew Henry

If pleasing people is your goal, you will
be enslaved to them. People can be harsh taskmasters
when you give them this power over you.
Sarah Young

Praise opens the window of our hearts, preparing us to walk
more closely with God. Prayer raises the window of our spirit,
enabling us to listen more clearly to the Father.
Max Lucado

When there is peace in the heart, there will be praise on the lips.
Warren Wiersbe

Praise God, from whom all blessings flow; praise Him,
all creatures here below; praise Him above, ye heav'nly host;
praise Father, Son, and Holy Ghost!
Thomas Ken

More from God's Word

Great is the LORD! He is most worthy of praise!
No one can measure his greatness.
PSALM 145:3 NLT

In everything give thanks;
for this is the will of God in Christ Jesus for you.
1 THESSALONIANS 5:18 NKJV

At the name of Jesus every knee should bow,
of things in heaven, and things in earth,
and things under the earth;
and that every tongue should confess that
Jesus Christ is Lord, to the glory of God the Father.
PHILIPPIANS 2:10–11 KJV

The LORD is my strength and my song;
He has become my salvation.
EXODUS 15:2 HCSB

From the rising of the sun to its setting
the name of the LORD is to be praised.
PSALM 113:3 NASB

Remember This

It always pays to praise your Creator. That's why thoughtful believers (like you) make it a habit to carve out quiet moments throughout the day to praise God.

59

THE PROMISE: BECAUSE THE LORD IS FAITHFUL, YOU CAN THINK OPTIMISTICALLY

The LORD is my light and my salvation—
whom should I fear? The LORD is the stronghold
of my life—of whom should I be afraid?
PSALM 27:1 HCSB

God's Word promises that you, like all of His children, possess the ability to experience earthy peace and spiritual abundance. Yet sometimes—especially if you dwell upon the inevitable disappointments that may, at times, befall even the most fortunate among us—you may allow pessimism to invade your thoughts and your heart. The nineteenth-century American poet Ella Wheeler Wilcox wrote a poem entitled "Optimism" in which she advised, "Say that you are well and all is well with you, and God will hear your words and make them true." Wilcox understood that optimism is, most often, a matter of intention. If you make the decision to think optimistically—if you purposefully direct your thoughts in positive directions—then you'll enhance your chances of achieving success.

The self-fulfilling prophecy is alive, well, and living at your house. If you constantly anticipate the worst, that's what you're likely to attract. But if you make the effort to think positive thoughts, you'll increase the probability that those positive thoughts will come true.

So here's a simple, time-tested tip for improving your life: Put the self-fulfilling prophecy to work for you. Expect the best, and then get busy working to achieve it. When you do, you'll not only increase the odds of achieving your dreams, but you'll also have more fun along the way.

More Thoughts about Optimism

Two types of voices command your attention today. Negative ones fill your mind with doubt, bitterness, and fear. Positive ones purvey hope and strength. Which one will you choose to heed?
Max Lucado

No more imperfect thoughts. No more sad memories. No more ignorance. My redeemed body will have a redeemed mind. Grant me a foretaste of that perfect mind as you mirror your thoughts in me today.
Joni Eareckson Tada

All things work together for good. Fret not, nor fear!
Lettie Cowman

Developing a positive attitude means working continually to find what is uplifting and encouraging.
Barbara Johnson

More from God's Word

Make me to hear joy and gladness.
PSALM 51:8 KJV

*But if we look forward to something we don't yet have,
we must wait patiently and confidently.*
ROMANS 8:25 NLT

*"I say this because I know what I am planning for you,"
says the LORD. "I have good plans for you, not plans to hurt you.
I will give you hope and a good future."*
JEREMIAH 29:11 NCV

*This hope we have as an anchor of the soul,
a hope both sure and steadfast.*
HEBREWS 6:19 NASB

*Let us hold on to the confession of our hope without
wavering, for He who promised is faithful.*
HEBREWS 10:23 HCSB

A Timely Tip

Be a realistic optimist. Your attitude toward the future will help create your future. So think realistically about yourself and your situation while making a conscious effort to focus on hopes, not fears.

60

THE PROMISE: WHEN YOU'RE SELF-DISCIPLINED, YOUR EFFORTS WILL BE REWARDED

Discipline yourself for the purpose of godliness.
1 TIMOTHY 4:7 NASB

God's Word reminds us again and again that our Creator expects us to lead disciplined lives. God doesn't reward laziness, misbehavior, or apathy. To the contrary, He expects us to behave with dignity and discipline. But ours is a world in which dignity and discipline are often in short supply.

We live in a world in which leisure is glorified and indifference is often glamorized. But God has other plans. God gives us talents, and He expects us to use them. But cultivating our talents is seldom easy. Sometimes we must invest countless hours (or, in some cases, many years) honing our skills. And that's perfectly okay with God, because He understands that self-discipline is a blessing, not a burden.

When we pause to consider how much work needs to be done,

we realize that self-discipline is not simply a proven way to get ahead; it's also an integral part of God's plan for our lives. If we genuinely seek to be faithful stewards of our time, our talents, and our resources, we must adopt a disciplined approach to life. Otherwise, our talents are wasted and our resources are squandered.

Life's greatest rewards seldom fall into our laps; to the contrary, our greatest accomplishments usually require work, perseverance, and discipline. May we, as disciplined believers, be willing to work toward the rewards we so earnestly desire.

More Thoughts about Self-Discipline

If one examines the secret behind a championship football team, a magnificent orchestra, or a successful business, the principal ingredient is invariably discipline.
James Dobson

Personal humility is a spiritual discipline and the hallmark of the service of Jesus.
Franklin Graham

The alternative to discipline is disaster.
Vance Havner

Think of something you ought to do and go do it. Heed not your feelings. Do your work.
George MacDonald

More from God's Word

Whatever you do, do your work heartily,
as for the Lord rather than for men.
COLOSSIANS 3:23 NASB

Better to be patient than powerful;
better to have self-control than to conquer a city.
PROVERBS 16:32 NLT

But the fruit of the Spirit is love, joy, peace,
patience, kindness, goodness, faith, gentleness,
self-control. Against such things there is no law.
GALATIANS 5:22–23 HCSB

Finishing is better than starting.
Patience is better than pride.
ECCLESIASTES 7:8 NLT

A final word: Be strong in the Lord
and in his mighty power.
EPHESIANS 6:10 NLT

Remember This

A disciplined lifestyle gives you more control over the inevitable ups and downs of everyday life. The more disciplined you become, the sooner you'll begin to assert control over your circumstances (which, by the way, is far better than letting your circumstances take control of you).

61

THE PROMISE: THE LORD REWARDS OBEDIENCE

For the eyes of the Lord are over the righteous,
and his ears are open unto their prayers:
but the face of the Lord is against them that do evil.
1 PETER 3:12 KJV

Since God created Adam and Eve, we human beings have been rebelling against our Creator. Why? Because we are unwilling to trust God's Word, and we are unwilling to follow His commandments. God has given us a guidebook for righteous living called the Holy Bible. It contains thorough instructions that, if followed, lead to fulfillment, abundance, and salvation. But if we choose to ignore God's commandments, the results are as predictable as they are tragic.

Obedience is determined, not by words, but by deeds. Talking about righteousness is easy; living righteously is far more difficult, especially in today's temptation-filled world.

But the good news is this: when we obey God, and when we spend time with friends who do the same, we enjoy profound spiritual rewards.

Do you seek the Lord's peace and His blessings? Then obey Him. When you're faced with a difficult choice or a powerful temptation, seek God's counsel and trust the counsel He gives. Invite God into your heart and live according to His commandments. When you do, you will be blessed today, and tomorrow, and forever.

More Thoughts about Obedience

*The golden rule for understanding
in spiritual matters is not intellect, but obedience.*
Oswald Chambers

Obedience is the key to every door.
George MacDonald

*Faith and obedience are bound up in the same bundle.
He that obeys God, trusts God;
and he that trusts God, obeys God.*
C. H. Spurgeon

*God has laid down spiritual laws which,
if obeyed, bring harmony and fulfillment,
but, if disobeyed, bring discord and disorder.*
Billy Graham

*Obedience is a foundational stepping-stone
on the path of God's will.*
Elizabeth George

More from God's Word

Now by this we know that we know Him,
if we keep His commandments.
1 JOHN 2:3 NKJV

We must obey God rather than men.
ACTS 5:29 NASB

Teach me, O LORD, the way of Your statutes,
and I shall observe it to the end.
PSALM 119:33 NASB

Trust in the LORD with all your heart,
and lean not on your own understanding; in all your ways
acknowledge Him, and He shall direct your paths.
PROVERBS 3:5–6 NKJV

Praise the LORD! Happy are those who respect the LORD,
who want what he commands.
PSALM 112:1 NCV

A Timely Tip

Obedience leads to spiritual growth. Oswald Chambers correctly observed, "We grow spiritually by a life of simple, unobtrusive obedience." When you take these words to heart, you will embark upon a life-altering spiritual journey.

62

THE PROMISE: GOD WANTS YOU TO CELEBRATE LIFE

This is the day the LORD has made;
let us rejoice and be glad in it.
PSALM 118:24 HCSB

The words of John 9:4 remind us that "night is coming" for all of us. But until then, God gives us each day and fills it to the brim with possibilities. The day is presented to us fresh and clean at midnight, free of charge, but we must beware: today is a nonrenewable resource— once it's gone, it's gone forever. Our responsibility, of course, is to use this day in the service of God's will and in accordance with His commandments.

Today is a priceless gift that has been given to you by God—don't waste it. Don't stand on the sidelines as life's parade passes you by. Instead, search for the hidden possibilities that the Lord has placed along your path. This day is a one-of-a-kind treasure that can be put to good use—or not. Your challenge is to use this day joyfully and productively. And while you're at it, encourage others to do likewise. After all, night is coming when no one can work.

More Thoughts about God's Gift of Today

Yesterday is the tomb of time,
and tomorrow is the womb of time.
Only now is yours.
R. G. Lee

Today is mine. Tomorrow is none of my business.
If I peer anxiously into the fog of the future,
I will strain my spiritual eyes so that
I will not see clearly what is required of me now.
Elisabeth Elliot

Each day is God's gift of a fresh
unspoiled opportunity to live
according to His priorities.
Elizabeth George

Faith does not concern itself
with the entire journey.
One step is enough.
Lettie Cowman

The one word in the spiritual vocabulary is now.
Oswald Chambers

More from God's Word

But encourage each other every day while
it is "today." Help each other so none of you will
become hardened because sin has tricked you.
HEBREWS 3:13 NCV

So don't worry about tomorrow,
because tomorrow will have its own worries.
Each day has enough trouble of its own.
MATTHEW 6:34 NCV

There is a time for everything,
and a season for every activity under the heavens.
ECCLESIASTES 3:1 NIV

The world and its desires pass away,
but whoever does the will of God lives forever.
1 JOHN 2:17 NIV

So teach us to number our days,
that we may present to You a heart of wisdom.
PSALM 90:12 NASB

A Timely Tip

Today is a wonderful, one-of-a-kind gift from God. Treat it that way.

63

THE PROMISE: THE LORD IS ALWAYS WITH YOU

I am not alone,
because the Father is with Me.
JOHN 16:32 NKJV

God is everywhere. He is everywhere you've ever been and everywhere you'll ever be. God is not "out there"; He is "right here," continuously reshaping His universe and continuously reshaping the lives of those who dwell in it. Your Creator is always listening to your thoughts and prayers, watching over your every move.

If difficult times are weighing heavy upon your heart, you may be tempted to ignore God's presence or—worse yet—to lose faith in His promises. But when you quiet yourself and acknowledge His presence, the Lord will touch your heart and renew your strength.

Psalm 46:10 remind us to "Be still, and know that I am God." When we do, we can be comforted in the knowledge that God does not love us from a distance. He is not just near. He is here.

MORE THOUGHTS ABOUT
GOD'S PRESENCE

There is a basic urge: the longing for unity.
You desire a reunion with God—
with God your Father.

E. STANLEY JONES

The next time you hear a baby laugh
or see an ocean wave, take note.
Pause and listen as His Majesty
whispers ever so gently, "I'm here."

MAX LUCADO

No matter what trials we face,
Christ never leaves us.

BILLY GRAHAM

The real test of being in the presence of God
is that you either forget about yourself altogether
or see yourself as a very small object.
It is better to forget about yourself altogether.

C. S. LEWIS

Get yourself into the presence of the loving Father.
Just place yourself before Him, and look up into
His face; think of His love,
His wonderful, tender, pitying love.

ANDREW MURRAY

More from God's Word

For the eyes of Yahweh roam throughout the earth
to show Himself strong for
those whose hearts are completely His.
2 Chronicles 16:9 HCSB

Draw near to God,
and He will draw near to you.
James 4:8 HCSB

I know the Lord is always with me.
I will not be shaken, for he is right beside me.
Psalm 16:8 NLT

Though I walk through the valley of the shadow of death,
I will fear no evil: for thou art with me.
Psalm 23:4 KJV

The Lord sees everything you do,
and he watches where you go.
Proverbs 5:21 NCV

A Timely Tip

Having trouble hearing God? If so, slow yourself down, tune out the distractions, and listen carefully. God has important things to say; your task is to be still and listen.

64

THE PROMISE: THE LORD WANTS YOU TO FOCUS ON HIS PATH FOR YOUR LIFE

*You reveal the path of life to me; in Your presence
is abundant joy; in Your right hand are eternal pleasures.*
PSALM 16:11 HCSB

What is your focus today? Are you willing to focus your thoughts and energies on God's blessings and upon His plan for your life? Or will you turn your thoughts to other things? Before you answer, consider this: The Lord created you in His own image, and He wants you to experience joy and abundance. But He will not force His joy upon you; you must claim it for yourself.

If you're experiencing difficult times, you may be tempted to focus on the more negative aspects of life. But to do so is shortsighted and counterproductive. After all, the Lord has promised to be your shepherd on good days and difficult days. And with Him as your protector, you have nothing, absolutely nothing, to fear.

This day—and every day hereafter—is a chance to celebrate the life that God has given you. It is also a chance to give thanks to the One who has offered you more blessings than you can possibly count. So today, as you seek God's guidance for the challenges ahead, focus on His love for you. Ask Him for wisdom and answer His call. With the Lord as your partner, you'll have every reason to think optimistically about yourself and your world. And you can then share your optimism with others. They'll be better for it, and so will you. But not necessarily in that order.

MORE THOUGHTS ABOUT FOCUS

Let's face it. None of us can do a thousand things to the glory of God. And, in our own vain attempt to do so, we stand the risk of forfeiting a precious thing.
BETH MOORE

Give me a person who says, "This one thing I do," and not "These fifty things I dabble in."
D. L. MOODY

Energy and time are limited entities. Therefore, we need to use them wisely, focusing on what is truly important.
SARAH YOUNG

It is important to set goals because if you do not have a plan, a goal, a direction, a purpose, and a focus, you are not going to accomplish anything for the glory of God.
BILL BRIGHT

There is nothing quite as potent as a focused life, one lived on purpose.
RICK WARREN

More from God's Word

Let your eyes look forward; fix your gaze straight ahead.
PROVERBS 4:25 HCSB

Therefore don't worry about tomorrow, because tomorrow will worry about itself. Each day has enough trouble of its own.
MATTHEW 6:34 HCSB

One thing I do, forgetting those things which are behind and reaching forward to those things which are ahead, I press toward the goal for the prize of the upward call of God in Christ Jesus.
PHILIPPIANS 3:13–14 NKJV

Get wisdom—how much better it is than gold! And get understanding—it is preferable to silver.
PROVERBS 16:16 HCSB

Trust in the LORD with all your heart, and lean not on your own understanding; in all your ways acknowledge Him, and He shall direct your paths.
PROVERBS 3:5–6 NKJV

A Timely Tip

Ask yourself if you're truly focusing your thoughts and energies on matters that are pleasing to God and beneficial to your family. Then ask your Creator to help you focus on His love, His Son, and His plan for your life.

65

THE PROMISE:
HIS KINGDOM'S WORK
IS FULFILLED
BY ACTION, NOT TALK

For the kingdom of God is not a matter of talk but of power.
1 CORINTHIANS 4:20 HCSB

The old saying is both familiar and true: actions speak louder than words. And as believers, we must beware: our actions should always give credence to the changes that Christ can make in the lives of those who walk with Him.

God calls upon each of us to act in accordance with His will and with respect for His commandments. If we are to be responsible believers, we must realize that it is never enough to hear the instructions of God; we must also live by them. And it is never enough to wait idly by while others do God's work here on earth; we, too, must act. Doing God's work is a responsibility that each of us must bear moment by moment and day by day.

Are you in the habit of doing what needs to be done when it needs to be done? If you've acquired the habit of doing things sooner rather than later, congratulations! But if you find yourself putting off all those unpleasant tasks until later (or never), it's time to think about the consequences of your behavior.

One way that you can learn to defeat procrastination is by paying less attention to your fears and more attention to your responsibilities. So when you're faced with a difficult choice or an unpleasant responsibility, don't spend endless hours fretting over your fate. Simply seek God's counsel and get busy. When you do, you will be richly rewarded because of your willingness to act.

More Thoughts about Taking Action Now

Every time you refuse to face up to life and its problems, you weaken your character.
E. STANLEY JONES

Every difficult task that comes across your path—every one that you would rather not do, that will take the most effort, cause the most pain, and be the greatest struggle—brings a blessing with it.
LETTIE COWMAN

If doing a good act in public will excite others to do more good, then "Let your light shine to all." Miss no opportunity to do good.
JOHN WESLEY

Now is the only time worth having because, indeed, it is the only time we have.
C. H. SPURGEON

More from God's Word

Therefore, with your minds ready for action,
be serious and set your hope completely on the grace
to be brought to you at the revelation of Jesus Christ.
1 Peter 1:13 HCSB

Whenever we have the opportunity, we should do good
to everyone—especially to those in the family of faith.
Galatians 6:10 NLT

When you make a vow to God, do not delay to fulfill it.
He has no pleasure in fools; fulfill your vow.
Ecclesiastes 5:4 NIV

Well done, good and faithful servant; you were
faithful over a few things, I will make you ruler
over many things. Enter into the joy of your lord.
Matthew 25:21 NKJV

But prove yourselves doers of the word,
and not merely hearers who delude themselves.
James 1:22 NASB

A Timely Tip

Today, pick out one important obligation that you've been putting off. Then take at least one specific step toward the completion of the task you've been avoiding. Even if you don't finish the job, you'll discover that it's easier to finish a job that you've already begun than to finish a job that you've never started.

66

THE PROMISE: ANGER IS CORROSIVE

Everyone must be quick to hear, slow to speak, and slow to anger, for man's anger does not accomplish God's righteousness.
JAMES 1:19–20 HCSB

During difficult times, minor frustrations can sometimes get the better of us. As the irritations mount, we may allow minor disappointments to cause us major problems. If we allow ourselves to become overly annoyed by the inevitable ups and downs of life, we may become overstressed, overheated, overanxious, or just plain angry.

Anger often leads to impulsivity; impulsivity often leads to poor decision making; and poor decisions can lead to big problems. So if you'd like to increase your storehouse of wisdom while at the same time improving the quality of your life, you must learn to control your temper before your temper controls you.

When you allow yourself to become angry, you are certain to defeat at least one person: yourself. When you allow the minor frustrations of everyday life to hijack your emotions, you do harm to yourself and to your loved ones. So today and every day, guard yourself against the kind of angry thinking that inevitably takes a toll on your emotions and your relationships. Don't allow feelings of anger or frustration to rule your life, or, for that matter, your day. Your life is simply too short for that, and you deserve much better treatment than that *from yourself.*

More Thoughts about Anger

Anger is the noise of the soul; the unseen irritant
of the heart; the relentless invader of silence.
MAX LUCADO

Bitterness and anger, usually over trivial things,
make havoc of homes, churches, and friendships.
WARREN WIERSBE

We must meet our disappointments,
our malicious enemies, our provoking friends,
our trials of every sort, with an attitude
of surrender and trust. We must rise above them
in Christ so they lose their power to harm us.
HANNAH WHITALL SMITH

Anger is the fluid that love bleeds when you cut it.
C. S. LEWIS

Anger breeds remorse in the heart,
discord in the home, bitterness in the community,
and confusion in the state.
BILLY GRAHAM

MORE FROM GOD'S WORD

But I tell you that anyone who is angry with his brother or sister will be subject to judgment.
MATTHEW 5:22 NIV

He who is slow to wrath has great understanding, but he who is impulsive exalts folly.
PROVERBS 14:29 NKJV

A hot-tempered man stirs up conflict, but a man slow to anger calms strife.
PROVERBS 15:18 HCSB

But now you must also put away all the following: anger, wrath, malice, slander, and filthy language from your mouth.
COLOSSIANS 3:8 HCSB

Do not let the sun go down on your anger, and do not give the devil an opportunity.
EPHESIANS 4:26–27 NASB

A TIMELY TIP

If you think you're about to explode in anger, don't! Instead of responding angrily, it's usually better to slow down, catch your breath, consider your options, and walk away if you must. Striking out in anger can lead to big problems. So it's better to walk away—and keep walking—than to blurt out angry words that can't be un-blurted.

67

THE PROMISE:
THE LORD CAN TURN
YOUR DISAPPOINTMENTS
INTO TRIUMPHS

Many adversities come to the one who is righteous,
but the LORD delivers him from them all.
PSALM 34:19 HCSB

As we make the journey from the cradle to the grave, disappointments are inevitable. No matter how competent we are, no matter how fortunate, we still encounter circumstances that fall far short of our expectations. When tough times arrive, we have choices to make: we can feel sorry for ourselves or we can get angry or we can become depressed.

Or we can get busy praying about our problems and solving them.

When we are disheartened—on those cloudy days when our strength is sapped and our hope is shaken—there exists a source from which we can draw perspective and courage. That source is God. When we turn everything over to Him, we find that He is sufficient to meet our needs. No problem is too big for Him.

So the next time you feel discouraged, slow down long enough to have a serious talk with your Creator. Pray for guidance, pray for strength, and pray for the wisdom to trust your heavenly Father. Your troubles are temporary; His love is not.

More Thoughts about Dealing with Disappointments

We all have sorrows and disappointments, but one must never forget that, if commended to God, they will issue in good. His own solution is far better than any we could conceive.
Fanny Crosby

Unless we learn to deal with disappointment, it will rob us of joy and poison our souls.
Billy Graham

If your hopes are being disappointed just now, it means that they are being purified.
Oswald Chambers

Discouragement is the opposite of faith. It is Satan's device to thwart the work of God in your life.
Billy Graham

Let God enlarge you when you are going through distress. He can do it.
Warren Wiersbe

More from God's Word

Then they cried out to the LORD in their trouble,
and He saved them out of their distresses.
PSALM 107:13 NKJV

He heals the brokenhearted
and binds up their wounds.
PSALM 147:3 HCSB

He shall not be afraid of evil tidings:
his heart is fixed, trusting in the LORD.
PSALM 112:7 KJV

My son, do not despise the chastening
of the LORD, nor be discouraged
when you are rebuked by Him.
HEBREWS 12:5 NKJV

They that sow in tears shall reap in joy.
PSALM 126:5 KJV

A Timely Tip

If you're feeling discouraged, try to redirect your thoughts away from the troubles that plague you—focus, instead, upon the opportunities that surround you.

68

THE PROMISE: PERSEVERANCE PAYS

*For you need endurance, so that after you have
done God's will, you may receive what was promised.*
HEBREWS 10:36 NASB

The next time you find your courage tested to the limit, remember that it pays to persevere. And remember that life's greatest victories are usually reserved for determined people (like you) who simply refuse to give up.

Occasionally, good things happen with little or no effort. Somebody wins the lottery or inherits a fortune or stumbles onto a financial bonanza by being at the right place at the right time. But more often than not, good things happen to people who work hard, and keep working hard, when just about everybody else has gone home or given up.

Calvin Coolidge observed, "Nothing in the world can take the place of persistence. Talent will not; genius will not; education will not. Persistence and determination alone are omnipotent." And President Coolidge was right. Perseverance pays.

Every marathon has a finish line, and so does yours. So keep putting one foot in front of the other, pray for strength, and don't give up. Whether you realize it or not, you're up to the challenge if you persevere. And with God's help, that's exactly what you'll do.

Perhaps you are in a hurry for God to help you resolve your difficulties. Perhaps you're anxious to earn the rewards that you feel you've already earned from life. Perhaps you're drumming your fingers, impatiently waiting for God to act. If so, be forewarned: God operates on His own timetable, not yours. Sometimes the Lord may answer your prayers with silence, and when He does, you must patiently persevere. In times of trouble, you must remain steadfast and trust in the merciful goodness of your heavenly Father. Whatever your problem, He can manage it. Your job is to keep persevering until He does.

More Thoughts about Perseverance

Jesus taught that perseverance is the essential element in prayer.
E. M. Bounds

Perseverance is more than endurance. It is endurance combined with absolute assurance and certainty that what we are looking for is going to happen.
Oswald Chambers

Battles are won in the trenches, in the grit and grime of courageous determination; they are won day by day in the arena of life.
Charles Swindoll

Don't quit. For if you do, you may miss the answer to your prayers.
Max Lucado

More from God's Word

Let us not become weary in doing good,
for at the proper time we will
reap a harvest if we do not give up.
GALATIANS 6:9 NIV

But as for you, be strong; don't be discouraged,
for your work has a reward.
2 CHRONICLES 15:7 HCSB

We are hard-pressed on every side, yet not crushed;
we are perplexed, but not in despair.
2 CORINTHIANS 4:8 NKJV

Finishing is better than starting.
Patience is better than pride.
ECCLESIASTES 7:8 NLT

So let us run the race that is before us and never give up.
We should remove from our lives anything that would
get in the way and the sin that so easily holds us back.
HEBREWS 12:1 NCV

A Timely Tip

Whenever you are being tested, you can call upon God, and you should. The Lord can give you the strength to persevere, and that's precisely what you should ask Him to do.

69

THE PROMISE:
IT PAYS TO BE THANKFUL

Enter into His gates with thanksgiving,
and into His courts with praise.
Be thankful to Him, and bless His name.
For the LORD is good; His mercy is everlasting,
and His truth endures to all generations.

PSALM 100:4–5 NKJV

As Christians, we are blessed beyond measure. God sent His only Son to die for our sins. And the Lord has given us the priceless gifts of eternal love and eternal life. We, in turn, are instructed to approach our heavenly Father with reverence and thanksgiving. But when we encounter difficult circumstances—or when we're caught up in the crush of our everyday responsibilities—we may not stop long enough to pause and thank our Creator for the countless blessings He has bestowed upon us.

When we slow down and express our gratitude to the One who made us, we enrich our own lives and the lives of those around us. Therefore, thanksgiving should become a habit, a regular part of our daily routines.

Do you appreciate the gifts that God has given you? And do you demonstrate your gratitude by being a faithful steward of the gifts and talents that you have received from your Creator? You most certainly should be thankful. After all, when you stop to think about it, God has given you more blessings than you can count. So the question of the day is this: will you thank your heavenly Father, or will you spend your time and energy doing other things?

God is always listening—are you willing to say thanks? It's up to you, and the next move is yours.

More Thoughts about Thanksgiving

Fill up the spare moments of your life with praise and thanksgiving.
Sarah Young

Thanksgiving or complaining—these words express two contrasting attitudes of the souls of God's children. The soul that gives thanks can find comfort in everything; the soul that complains can find comfort in nothing.
Hannah Whitall Smith

Thanksgiving will draw our hearts out to God and keep us engaged with Him.
Andrew Murray

No matter what our circumstance, we can find a reason to be thankful.
David Jeremiah

It is only with gratitude that life becomes rich.
Dietrich Bonhoeffer

More from God's Word

And whatever you do, in word or in deed,
do everything in the name of the Lord Jesus,
giving thanks to God the Father through Him.
Colossians 3:17 HCSB

Rejoice always, pray without ceasing,
in everything give thanks; for this is
the will of God in Christ Jesus for you.
1 Thessalonians 5:16–18 NKJV

Surely the righteous shall give thanks to Your name;
the upright shall dwell in Your presence.
Psalm 140:13 NKJV

I will thank Yahweh with all my heart;
I will declare all Your wonderful works.
I will rejoice and boast about You;
I will sing about Your name, Most High.
Psalm 9:1–2 HCSB

Thanks be to God for His indescribable gift.
2 Corinthians 9:15 HCSB

A Timely Tip

Since you're thankful for the Lord's blessings, tell Him so. And keep telling Him every day of your life.

70

THE PROMISE: WHEN YOU WALK WITH THE LORD, YOU WILL BE BLESSED

Blessed is the man who walks not in the counsel of the ungodly, nor stands in the path of sinners, nor sits in the seat of the scornful; but his delight is in the law of the LORD, and in His law he meditates day and night. He shall be like a tree planted by the rivers of water, that brings forth its fruit in its season, whose leaf also shall not wither; and whatever he does shall prosper.

PSALM 1:1–3 NKJV

God's Word makes it clear: integrity matters to Him, so it must also matter to us. If we wish to walk in the light of God's truth, we must be truthful. Honesty enriches relationships; deception destroys them.

Henry Blackaby observed, "God is interested in developing your character. At times He lets you proceed, but He will never let you go too far without discipline to bring you back." The implication is clear: personal integrity is important to God, so it must be important to us.

When you experience tough times, your character may be tested, perhaps to the limit. When you encounter difficult circumstances, you may discover that living a life of integrity isn't the easiest way.

But when you guard your integrity as carefully as you guard your wallet, you'll feel better about yourself, and you'll be blessed because of your obedience.

So if you ever find yourself tempted to bend the truth—or to break it—remember that honesty is, indeed, the best policy. It's also God's policy, so it must be your policy, too.

More Thoughts about Character

Before God changes our circumstances,
He wants to change our hearts.
Warren Wiersbe

Maintaining your integrity in a world
of sham is no small accomplishment.
Wayne Oates

Every time you refuse to face up to life
and its problems, you weaken your character.
E. Stanley Jones

No man can use his Bible with power unless
he has the character of Jesus in his heart.
Alan Redpath

Right actions done for the wrong reason do not help
to build the internal quality of character called a "virtue,"
and it is this quality or character that really matters.
C. S. Lewis

More from God's Word

Whoever walks in integrity walks securely,
but whoever takes crooked paths will be found out.
PROVERBS 10:9 NIV

The integrity of the upright guides them,
but the perversity of the treacherous destroys them.
PROVERBS 11:3 HCSB

The godly are directed by honesty.
PROVERBS 11:5 NLT

He stores up success for the upright;
He is a shield for those who live with integrity.
PROVERBS 2:7 HCSB

The godly walk with integrity;
blessed are their children who follow them.
PROVERBS 20:7 NLT

A Timely Tip

When your words are true and your intentions are pure, you have nothing to fear. God rewards integrity just as surely as He punishes duplicity. So you must never allow another person to bully you into doing something that God disapproves of.

71

THE PROMISE: WHEN YOU CAST YOUR BURDENS ON THE LORD, HE WILL SUSTAIN YOU

Cast your burden on the LORD, and He shall sustain you;
He shall never permit the righteous to be moved.
PSALM 55:22 NKJV

Because you have the ability to think, you also have the ability to worry. Even if you're a very faithful Christian, you may be plagued by occasional periods of discouragement and doubt. Even though you trust God's promise of eternal life—even though you sincerely believe in God's love and protection—you may find yourself upset by the countless details of everyday life.

Where is the best place to take your worries? Take them to God. Take your troubles to Him; take your fears to Him; take your doubts to Him; take your weaknesses to Him; take your sorrows to Him . . . and leave them all there. Seek protection from the One who offers you eternal salvation; build your spiritual house upon the Rock that cannot be moved.

The very same God who created the universe has promised to

protect you now and forever. So what do you have to worry about? With God on your side, the answer is, nothing.

MORE THOUGHTS ABOUT
OVERCOMING WORRY

Much that worries us beforehand can, quite unexpectedly, have a happy and simple solution. Worries just don't matter. Things really are in a better hand than ours.
DIETRICH BONHOEFFER

The beginning of anxiety is the end of faith, and the beginning of true faith is the end of anxiety.
GEORGE MUELLER

With the peace of God to guard us and the God of peace to guide us—why worry?
WARREN WIERSBE

The more you meditate on God's Word, the less you will have to worry about.
RICK WARREN

Our fears for today, our worries about tomorrow, and even the powers of hell can't keep God's love away.
BILL BRIGHT

More from God's Word

Let not your heart be troubled;
you believe in God, believe also in Me.
JOHN 14:1 NKJV

Cast all your anxiety on him because he cares for you.
1 PETER 5:7 NIV

Peace I leave with you; My peace I give to you;
not as the world gives do I give to you.
Do not let your heart be troubled, nor let it be fearful.
JOHN 14:27 NASB

Do not be anxious about anything,
but in every situation, by prayer and petition,
with thanksgiving, present your requests to God.
PHILIPPIANS 4:6 NIV

Let us hold tightly without wavering to the hope we affirm,
for God can be trusted to keep his promise.
HEBREWS 10:23 NLT

A Timely Tip

Assiduously divide your areas of concern into two categories: those you can control and those you cannot control. Then focus on the former and resolve never to waste time or energy worrying about the latter.

72

THE PROMISE: WHEN YOUR PERSPECTIVE IS RIGHT, YOU'LL BE AT PEACE

Joyful is the person who finds wisdom,
the one who gains understanding.
PROVERBS 3:13 NLT

For most of us, life is busy and complicated. Amid the rush and crush of the daily grind, it is easy to lose perspective—easy, but wrong. When the world seems to be spinning out of control, we can regain perspective by slowing ourselves down and then turning our thoughts and prayers toward God.

The familiar words of Psalm 46:10 remind us to "be still, and know that I am God" (NKJV). When we do so, we are reminded of God's love (not to mention God's priorities), and we can then refocus our thoughts on the things that matter most. But when we ignore the presence of our Creator—if we rush from place to place with scarcely a spare minute for God—we rob ourselves of His perspective, His peace, and His joy.

Do you carve out quiet moments each day to offer thanksgiving and praise to your Creator? You should. During these moments, you will often sense the love and wisdom of our Lord. So today and every day, make time to be still before God. When you do, you can face the day's complications with the wisdom, the perspective, and the power that only He can provide.

MORE THOUGHTS ABOUT PERSPECTIVE

What you see and hear depends a good deal on where you are standing; it also depends on what sort of person you are.
C. S. LEWIS

When you and I hurt deeply, what we really need is not an explanation from God but a revelation of God. We need to see how great God is; we need to recover our lost perspective on life. Things get out of proportion when we are suffering, and it takes a vision of something bigger than ourselves to get life's dimensions adjusted again.
WARREN WIERSBE

Joy is the direct result of having God's perspective on our daily lives and the effect of loving our Lord enough to obey His commands and trust His promises.
BILL BRIGHT

Perspective is everything when you are experiencing the challenges of life.
JONI EARECKSON TADA

More from God's Word

If you teach the wise, they will get knowledge.
PROVERBS 21:11 NCV

The one who acquires good sense loves himself;
one who safeguards understanding finds success.
PROVERBS 19:8 HCSB

Since you have been raised to new life with Christ,
set your sights on the realities of heaven, where Christ
sits in the place of honor at God's right hand.
COLOSSIANS 3:1 NLT

Teach me, LORD, the meaning of Your statutes,
and I will always keep them.
PSALM 119:33 HCSB

Trust in the LORD with all your heart
and lean not on your own understanding.
PROVERBS 3:5 NIV

A Timely Tip

Keep life in perspective. Remember that your life is an integral part of God's grand plan. So don't become unduly upset over the minor inconveniences of life, and don't worry too much about today's setbacks—they're temporary.

73

THE PROMISE:
GOD IS LOVE

*And we have known and believed the love
that God has for us. God is love, and he who
abides in love abides in God, and God in him.*

1 JOHN 4:16 NKJV

God loves you so much that He sent His Son Jesus to come to this earth to die for you. Now, precisely because you are a wondrous creation treasured by God, a few questions are in order: What will you do in response to God's love? Will you ignore it or embrace it? Will you return it or neglect it? Will you receive it and share it . . . or not? The answer to these simple questions will determine the level of your faith and the quality of your life.

When you form the habit of embracing God's love day in and day out, you will feel differently about yourself, your neighbors, and your world. When you embrace God's love, you will share His message and you His commandments.

God's heart is overflowing with love for you and yours. Accept that love. Return that love. Respect that love. And share that love. Today.

More Thoughts about God's Love

If you have an obedience problem,
you have a love problem.
Focus your attention on God's love.
HENRY BLACKABY

Even when we cannot see the why
and wherefore of God's dealings,
we know that there is love in and behind them,
so we can rejoice always.
J. I. PACKER

The love of God is one of the great realities
of the universe, a pillar upon which
the hope of the world rests. But it is a personal,
intimate thing too. God does not love populations.
He loves people. He loves not masses, but men.
A. W. TOZER

God proved His love on the cross.
BILLY GRAHAM

There is no pit so deep that God's love is not deeper still.
CORRIE TEN BOOM

More from God's Word

We love him, because he first loved us.
1 JOHN 4:19 KJV

For He is gracious and compassionate,
slow to anger, rich in faithful love.
JOEL 2:13 HCSB

For God so loved the world, that he gave
his only begotten Son, that whosoever believeth
in him should not perish, but have everlasting life.
JOHN 3:16 KJV

Give thanks to Him and praise His name.
For Yahweh is good, and His love is eternal;
His faithfulness endures through all generations.
PSALM 100:4–5 HCSB

The LORD's lovingkindnesses indeed never cease,
for His compassions never fail.
They are new every morning.
Great is Your faithfulness.
LAMENTATIONS 3:22–23 NASB

Remember This

When all else fails, God's love does not. You can always depend upon God's love, and He is always your ultimate protection.

74

THE PROMISE:
WHEN YOU QUIET
YOURSELF AND LISTEN
TO GOD, HE WILL SPEAK

The one who is from God listens to God's words.
This is why you don't listen, because you are not from God.
JOHN 8:47 HCSB

God speaks to us in different ways at different times. Sometimes He speaks loudly and clearly. But more often, He speaks in a quiet voice. And if you are wise, you will be listening carefully when He does. To do so, you must carve out quiet moments each day to study His Word and to sense His direction for your life.

Are you willing to pray sincerely and then to wait quietly for God's response? Can you quiet yourself long enough to listen to your conscience? Are you attuned to the subtle guidance of your intuition? Hopefully so. Usually God refrains from sending His messages on stone tablets or city billboards. More often, He communicates in subtler ways. If you sincerely desire to hear His voice, you must listen carefully, and you must do so in the silent corners of your quiet, willing heart.

More Thoughts about Listening to God

In the soul-searching of our lives,
we are to stay quiet so we can hear
Him say all that He wants to say to us in our hearts.
Charles Swindoll

Listening is loving.
Zig Ziglar

We cannot experience the fullness of Christ
if we do all the expressing. We must allow
God to express His love, will, and truth to us.
Gary Smalley

An essential condition of listening to God
is that the mind should not be distracted by thoughts of
resentment, ill-temper, hatred, or vengeance, all of which
are comprised in the general term, the wrath of man.
R. V. G. Tasker

In prayer, the ear is of first importance.
It is of equal importance with the tongue,
but the ear must be named first. We must listen to God.
S. D. Gordon

More from God's Word

Be still, and know that I am God.
PSALM 46:10 KJV

In quietness and in confidence shall be your strength.
ISAIAH 30:15 KJV

Rest in the LORD,
and wait patiently for Him.
PSALM 37:7 NKJV

Listen, listen to me, and eat what is good,
and you will delight in the richest of fare.
Give ear and come to me; listen, that you may live.
ISAIAH 55:2–3 NIV

Be silent before Me.
ISAIAH 41:1 HCSB

A Timely Tip

Today, take a few moments to consider the fact that prayer is two-way communication with God. Talking to God isn't enough; you should also listen to Him.

75

THE PROMISE: YOUR GOOD WORKS WILL BEAR FRUIT

But this I say: He who sows sparingly will also reap sparingly,
and he who sows bountifully will also reap bountifully.
2 CORINTHIANS 9:6 NKJV

The old adage is both familiar and true: We must pray as if everything depended upon the Lord, but work as if everything depended upon us. Yet sometimes, when we are weary or discouraged, we may allow our worries to sap our energy and our hope. God has other intentions. God intends that we pray for things, and He intends that we be willing to work for the things that we pray for. More importantly, God intends that our work become His work.

God has created a world in which diligence is rewarded and sloth is not. So whatever you choose to do, do it with commitment, with excitement, with enthusiasm, and with vigor.

In his second letter to the Thessalonians, Paul warns, "If any would not work, neither should he eat" (3:10 KJV). And the book of Proverbs proclaims, "One who is slack in his work is brother to one who destroys" (18:9 NIV). Clearly, God's Word commends the value and importance of diligence. Yet we live in a world that, all too often, glorifies leisure while downplaying the importance of shoulder-to-the wheel hard work. Rest assured, however, that God does not underestimate the value of diligence. And neither should you.

God did not create you to be ordinary; He created you for far greater things. Reaching for greater things usually requires work and lots of it, which is perfectly fine with the Lord. After all, He knows that you're up to the task, and He has big plans for you. Very big plans.

More Thoughts about Work

God did not intend for us to be idle
and unproductive. There is dignity in work.
Billy Graham

Pray as though everything depended on God.
Work as though everything depended on you.
St. Augustine

Ordinary work, which is what most of us
do most of the time, is ordained by God
every bit as much as is the extraordinary.
Elisabeth Elliot

It may be that the day of judgment will
dawn tomorrow; in that case, we shall gladly
stop working for a better future. But not before.
Dietrich Bonhoeffer

MORE FROM GOD'S WORD

Whatever you do, do it enthusiastically,
as something done for the Lord and not for men.
COLOSSIANS 3:23 HCSB

Be strong and courageous, and do the work.
Don't be afraid or discouraged, for the LORD God, my God,
is with you. He won't leave you or forsake you.
1 CHRONICLES 28:20 HCSB

The plans of hard-working people earn a profit,
but those who act too quickly become poor.
PROVERBS 21:5 NCV

Do you see a man skilled in his work?
He will stand in the presence of kings.
PROVERBS 22:29 HCSB

I must work the works of Him who sent Me while it is day;
the night is coming when no one can work.
JOHN 9:4 NKJV

A TIMELY TIP

Here's a time-tested formula for success: Have faith in God and do the work. Hard work is not simply a proven way to get ahead, it's also part of God's plan for all His children (including you).

76

THE PROMISE:
A HARDENED HEART
BEARS BITTER FRUIT

Let all bitterness, wrath, anger, clamor,
and evil speaking be put away from you, with all malice.
And be kind to one another, tenderhearted,
forgiving one another, just as God in Christ forgave you.
EPHESIANS 4:31–32 NKJV

Bitterness is a spiritual sickness. It will consume your soul; it is dangerous to your emotional health; it can destroy you if you let it. Don't let it.

The world holds few if any rewards for those who remain angrily focused upon the past. Still, the act of forgiveness is difficult for all but the most saintly men and women. Being frail, fallible, imperfect human beings, most of us are quick to anger, quick to blame, slow to forgive, and even slower to forget. Yet we know that it's best to forgive others, just as we, too, have been forgiven.

If there exists even one person—including yourself—against whom you still harbor bitter feelings, it's time to forgive and move on. Bitterness and regret are not part of God's plan for you, but God won't force you to forgive others. It's a job that only you can finish, and the sooner you finish it, the better.

If you are caught up in intense feelings of anger or resentment, you know all too well the destructive power of those emotions. How can you rid yourself of these feelings? First, you must prayerfully ask God to cleanse your heart. Then, you must learn to catch yourself whenever thoughts of bitterness or hatred begin to attack you. Your challenge is simply this: You must learn to resist negative thoughts before they hijack your emotions. When you learn to direct your thoughts toward more positive topics, you'll be protected from the spiritual and emotional consequences of bitterness. And you'll be wiser, healthier, and happier too.

MORE THOUGHTS ABOUT
MOVING BEYOND BITTERNESS

Bitterness imprisons life; love releases it.
HARRY EMERSON FOSDICK

Bitterness is anger gone sour, an attitude of deep discontent that poisons our souls and destroys our peace.
BILLY GRAHAM

Bitterness is the price we charge ourselves for being unwilling to forgive.
MARIE T. FREEMAN

Bitterness sentences you to relive the hurt over and over.
LEE STROBEL

More from God's Word

Do all things without complaining and disputing,
that you may become blameless and harmless, children
of God without fault in the midst of a crooked and perverse
generation, among whom you shine as lights in the world.
Philippians 2:14–15 NKJV

Do not repay anyone evil for evil.
Try to do what is honorable in everyone's eyes.
Romans 12:17 HCSB

But when you are praying, first forgive anyone
you are holding a grudge against, so that your
Father in heaven will forgive your sins, too.
Mark 11:25 NLT

The heart knows its own bitterness,
and a stranger does not share its joy.
Proverbs 14:10 NKJV

Do not judge, and you will not be judged.
Do not condemn, and you will not be condemned.
Forgive, and you will be forgiven.
Luke 6:37 HCSB

Remember This

You can never fully enjoy the present if you're bitter about the past.
So instead of living in the past, make peace with it and move on.

THE PROMISE: EVEN DURING DIFFICULT DAYS, WE ARE ACCOUNTABLE FOR OUR ACTIONS

*But each person should examine his own work,
and then he will have a reason for boasting in himself alone,
and not in respect to someone else.
For each person will have to carry his own load.*

GALATIANS 6:4–5 HCSB

We humans are masters at passing the buck. Why? Because *passing* the buck is easier than *fixing* the problem, and criticizing *others* is so much easier than improving *ourselves*. So instead of solving our problems legitimately (by doing the work required to solve them) we are inclined to fret, to blame, and to criticize, while doing precious little else. When we do, our problems, quite predictably, remain unsolved.

Whether you like it or not, you (and only you) are accountable for your actions. But because you are human, you may be tempted to pass the blame. Avoid that temptation at all costs.

Problem solving builds character. Every time you straighten your back and look squarely into the face of Old Man Trouble, you'll strengthen not only your backbone but also your spirit. So instead of looking for someone to blame, look for something to fix, and then get busy fixing it. And as you consider your own situation, remember this: God has a way of helping those who help themselves, but He doesn't spend much time helping those who don't.

MORE THOUGHTS
ABOUT ACCOUNTABILITY

*Generally speaking, accountability is a willingness
to share our activities, conduct,
and fulfillment of assigned responsibilities with others.*
CHARLES STANLEY

*One of the real tests of Christian character
is to be found in the lives we live from day to day.*
BILLY GRAHAM

*We urgently need people who encourage and inspire us to move
toward God and away from the world's enticing pleasures.*
JIM CYMBALA

*The Bible teaches that we are accountable
to one another for our conduct and character.*
CHARLES STANLEY

*Never fail to do something because
you don't feel like it. Sometimes you just have
to do it now, and you'll feel like it later.*
MARIE T. FREEMAN

More from God's Word

Now by this we know that we know Him,
if we keep His commandments.
1 John 2:3 NKJV

Walk in a manner worthy of the God who
calls you into His own kingdom and glory.
1 Thessalonians 2:12 NASB

Live peaceful and quiet lives
in all godliness and holiness.
1 Timothy 2:2 NIV

But prove yourselves doers of the word,
and not merely hearers who delude themselves.
James 1:22 NASB

In everything set them an example
by doing what is good.
Titus 2:7 NIV

A Timely Tip

It's easy to hold other people accountable, but real accountability begins with the person in the mirror. Think about one specific area of responsibility that is uniquely yours, and think about a specific step you can take today to better fulfill that responsibility.

78

THE PROMISE:
IF YOU STRIVE TO KEEP
YOUR CONSCIENCE CLEAR,
YOU WILL BE BLESSED

Now the goal of our instruction is love from
a pure heart, a good conscience, and a sincere faith.
1 TIMOTHY 1:5 HCSB

God has given each of us a conscience, and He intends for us to use it. But sometimes we don't. Instead of listening to that quiet inner voice that warns us against disobedience and danger, we're tempted to rush headlong into situations that we soon come to regret.

God promises that He rewards good conduct and that He blesses those who obey His Word. The Lord also issues a stern warning to those who rebel against His commandments. Wise men and women heed that warning. Count yourself among their number.

Sometime soon, perhaps today, your conscience will speak; when it does, listen carefully. God may be trying to get a message through to you. Don't miss it.

More Thoughts about Listening to Your Conscience

To go against one's conscience
is neither safe nor right.
Here I stand. I cannot do otherwise.
MARTIN LUTHER

Conscience is God's voice to the inner man.
BILLY GRAHAM

Conscience can only be satisfied if God is satisfied.
C. H. SPURGEON

God speaks through a variety of means.
In the present God primarily speaks
by the Holy Spirit, through the Bible,
prayer, circumstances, and the church.
HENRY BLACKABY

God desires that we become
spiritually healthy enough through faith
to have a conscience that rightly interprets
the work of the Holy Spirit.
BETH MOORE

More from God's Word

So I strive always to keep my conscience
clear before God and man.
Acts 24:16 NIV

Let us come near to God with a sincere heart
and a sure faith, because we have been
made free from a guilty conscience,
and our bodies have been washed with pure water.
Hebrews 10:22 NCV

People's thoughts can be like a deep well,
but someone with understanding
can find the wisdom there.
Proverbs 20:5 NCV

Create in me a clean heart, O God;
and renew a right spirit within me.
Psalm 51:10 KJV

Behold, the kingdom of God is within you.
Luke 17:21 KJV

A Timely Tip

The more important the decision, the more you should pray about it, and the more carefully you should listen to your conscience.

79

THE PROMISE: GOD GIVES STRENGTH

He gives strength to the weary,
and to him who lacks might He increases power.
ISAIAH 40:29 NASB

Today, like every other day, is brimming with possibilities. Whether we realize it or not, the Lord is always working in us and through us; our job is to lct Him do His work without undue interference. Yet we are imperfect beings who, because of our limited vision, often resist God's will. And oftentimes, because of our stubborn insistence on squeezing too many activities into a twenty-four-hour day, we allow ourselves to become exhausted or frustrated or both.

Are you tired or troubled? Turn your heart toward God in prayer. Are you weak or worried? Take the time—or more accurately, make the time—to delve deeply into God's holy Word. Are you spiritually depleted? Call upon fellow believers to support you, and call upon Christ to renew your spirit and your life. Are you simply overwhelmed by the demands of the day? Pray for the wisdom to simplify your life. Are you exhausted? Pray for the wisdom to rest a little more and worry a little less. When you do these things, you'll discover that the Creator of the universe stands always ready and always able to give you the strength you need to meet any challenge.

More Thoughts about Strength

Walking with God leads to receiving
His intimate counsel,
and counseling leads to deep restoration.
John Eldredge

Faith is a strong power, mastering
any difficulty in the strength of the Lord
who made heaven and earth.
Corrie ten Boom

The resurrection of Jesus Christ
is the power of God to change
history and to change lives.
Bill Bright

God will give us the strength
and resources we need to live through
any situation in life that He ordains.
Billy Graham

A divine strength is given to
those who yield themselves to the Father
and obey what He tells them to do.
Warren Wiersbe

More from God's Word

The LORD is my strength and my song;
He has become my salvation.
EXODUS 15:2 HCSB

My grace is sufficient for you,
for my power is made perfect in weakness.
2 CORINTHIANS 12:9 NIV

Have faith in the LORD your God, and you will stand strong.
Have faith in his prophets, and you will succeed.
2 CHRONICLES 20:20 NCV

Be strong and courageous, and do the work.
Don't be afraid or discouraged, for the LORD God,
my God, is with you. He won't leave you or forsake you.
1 CHRONICLES 28:20 HCSB

I can do all things through Christ who strengthens me.
PHILIPPIANS 4:13 NKJV

A Timely Tip

Need strength? Let God's Spirit reign over your heart: Anne Graham Lotz wrote, "The amount of power you experience to live a victorious, triumphant Christian life is directly proportional to the freedom you give the Spirit to be Lord of your life!" And remember that the best time to begin living triumphantly is the present moment.

80

THE PROMISE: THE LORD HAS A CALLING SPECIFICALLY DESIGNED FOR YOU

But as God has distributed to each one,
as the Lord has called each one, so let him walk.

1 CORINTHIANS 7:17 NKJV

The Lord is calling you to follow a specific path that He has chosen for your life. And it is vitally important that you heed that call. Otherwise, your talents and opportunities may go unused.

Have you already heard God's call? And are you pursuing it with vigor? If so, you're both fortunate and wise. But if you have not yet discovered what God intends for you to do with the rest of your life, keep searching and keep praying until you discover why the Creator put you here.

Remember: The Lord has important work for you to do—it's work that no one else on earth can accomplish but you. The Creator has placed you in a particular location, amid particular people, with unique opportunities to serve. And He has given you all the tools you need to succeed. So listen for His voice, watch for His signs, and prepare yourself for the call that is sure to come.

More Thoughts about God's Calling

*God will help us become the people
we are meant to be, if only we will ask Him.*
HANNAH WHITALL SMITH

*There's some task which the God of all the universe,
the great Creator has for you to do, and which will
remain undone and incomplete, until by faith
and obedience, you step into the will of God.*
ALAN REDPATH

*All of God's people are ordinary people
who have been made extraordinary
by the purpose He has given them.*
OSWALD CHAMBERS

*God never calls a person into
His service without equipping him.*
BILLY GRAHAM

*It's important that you keep asking God
to show you what He wants you to do.
If you don't ask, you won't know.*
STORMIE OMARTIAN

More from God's Word

I urge you to live a life worthy
of the calling you have received.
EPHESIANS 4:1 NIV

And we know that all things work together
for good to those who love God,
to those who are the called according to His purpose.
ROMANS 8:28 NKJV

For whoever does the will of God
is My brother and My sister and mother.
MARK 3:35 NKJV

For many are called, but few are chosen.
MATTHEW 22:14 KJV

For you have need of endurance,
so that when you have done the will of God,
you may receive what was promised.
HEBREWS 10:36 NASB

Remember This

God has a plan for your life, a divine calling that only you can fulfill.
How you choose to respond to His calling will determine the direction
you take and the contributions you make.

81

THE PROMISE: WHEN YOU TRUST GOD COMPLETELY, YOUR FUTURE IS BRIGHT

There is surely a future hope for you,
and your hope will not be cut off.
PROVERBS 23:18 NIV

If you've entrusted your heart to Christ, your eternal fate is secure and your future is eternally bright. No matter how troublesome your present circumstances may seem, you need not fear because the Lord has promised that you are His now and forever.

Of course, you won't be exempt from the normal challenges of life here on earth. While you're here, you'll probably experience your fair share of disappointments, emergencies, setbacks, and outright failures. But these are only temporary defeats.

Are you willing to place your future in the hands of a loving and all-knowing God? Do you trust in the ultimate goodness of His plan for you? Will you face today's challenges with hope and optimism? You should. After all, God created you for a very important purpose: His purpose. And you still have important work to do: His work. So today, as you live in the present and look to the future, remember that God has a marvelous plan for you. Act—and believe—accordingly.

More Thoughts about the Future

Never be afraid to trust an
unknown future to a known God.
Corrie ten Boom

Our future may look fearfully intimidating,
yet we can look up to the Engineer of the Universe,
confident that nothing escapes His attention
or slips out of the control of those strong hands.
Elisabeth Elliot

Knowing that your future is absolutely assured
can free you to live abundantly today.
Sarah Young

It may be that the day of judgment
will dawn tomorrow; in that case, we shall gladly
stop working for a better future. But not before.
Dietrich Bonhoeffer

Every experience God gives us, every person
He brings into our lives, is the perfect
preparation for the future that only He can see.
Corrie ten Boom

More from God's Word

"For I know the thoughts that I think toward you,"
says the LORD, "thoughts of peace and not of evil,
to give you a future and a hope. Then you will call upon Me
and go and pray to Me, and I will listen to you."
JEREMIAH 29:11–2 NKJV

The LORD is my light and my salvation—
whom should I fear? The LORD is the stronghold
of my life—of whom should I be afraid?
PSALM 27:1 HCSB

But if we look forward to something we don't yet have,
we must wait patiently and confidently.
ROMANS 8:25 NLT

Wisdom is pleasing to you. If you find it,
you have hope for the future.
PROVERBS 24:14 NCV

Rest in God alone, my soul, for my hope comes from Him.
PSALM 62:5 HCSB

A Timely Tip

Your future depends, to a very great extent, upon you. So keep learning and keep growing personally, intellectually, emotionally, and spiritually.

82

THE PROMISE:
THE GREATEST
OF THESE IS LOVE

And now abide faith, hope, love, these three;
but the greatest of these is love.
1 CORINTHIANS 13:13 NKJV

God is love, and He intends that we share His love with the world. But He won't force us to be loving and kind. He places that responsibility squarely on our shoulders.

Love, like everything else in this world, begins and ends with God, but the middle part belongs to us. The Creator gives each of us the opportunity to be kind, to be courteous, and to be loving. He gives each of us the chance to obey the Golden Rule, or to make up our own rules as we go. If we obey God's instructions, we're secure; but if we do otherwise, we suffer.

Christ's words are clear: "'Love the Lord your God with all your heart and with all your soul and with all your mind.' This is the first and greatest commandment. And the second is like it: 'Love your neighbor as yourself.' All the Law and the Prophets hang on these two commandments" (Matthew 22:37–40 NIV). We are commanded to love the One who first loved us and then to share His love with the world. And the next move is always ours.

MORE THOUGHTS ABOUT LOVE

Sacrificial love, giving-up love, is love that is willing to go to any lengths to provide for the well-being of the beloved.
ED YOUNG

Homes that are built on anything other than love are bound to crumble.
BILLY GRAHAM

It is when we come to the Lord in our nothingness, our powerlessnes, and our helplessness that He then enables us to love in a way which, without Him, would be absolutely impossible.
ELISABETH ELLIOT

Suppose that I understand the Bible. And, suppose that I am the greatest preacher who ever lived! The apostle Paul wrote that unless I have love, "I am nothing."
BILLY GRAHAM

Faith, like light, should always be simple and unbending; love, like warmth, should beam forth on every side and bend to every necessity of our brethren.
MARTIN LUTHER

More from God's Word

A new commandment I give unto you,
That ye love one another; as I have loved you,
that ye also love one another.

Love is patient, love is kind. Love does not envy,
is not boastful, is not conceited.
1 CORINTHIANS 13:4 HCSB

Beloved, if God so loved us,
we ought also to love one another.
1 JOHN 4:11 KJV

Above all, love each other deeply,
because love covers a multitude of sins.
1 PETER 4:8 NIV

And we have known and believed
the love that God has for us.
God is love, and he who abides in love
abides in God, and God in him.
1 JOHN 4:16 NKJV

Remember This

God loves you, and He wants you to reflect His love to those around you during happy times and trying times. In other words, it's always the right time to share God's love.

83

THE PROMISE:
IF YOU PUT GOD FIRST,
YOU WILL BE BLESSED

*No one can serve two masters. For you will hate one
and love the other; you will be devoted to one and despise
the other. You cannot serve God and be enslaved to money.*
LUKE 16:13 NLT

As you contemplate your own relationship with God, remember this: All of mankind is engaged in the practice of worship. Some people choose to worship the Lord and put Him first in their lives. As a result, they reap the joy that He offers to those who choose Him.

In the book of Exodus, God warns that we should place no gods before Him. Yet all too often, we place our Lord in second, third, or fourth place as we worship the gods of pride, greed, or power. When we place our desires for material possessions above our love for God—or when we yield to other temptations that the enemy places along our path—we find ourselves engaged in a struggle that is similar to the one Jesus faced when He was tempted by Satan. In the wilderness, Satan offered Jesus earthly power and unimaginable riches, but Jesus turned Satan away and chose instead to worship the Lord. We must do likewise by putting God first and worshiping only Him.

Does God rule your heart? Make certain that the honest answer to this question is a resounding yes. When you put God first and follow in the footsteps of His Son, you are secure, now and forever.

MORE THOUGHTS ABOUT PUTTING GOD FIRST

The most important thing you must decide
to do every day is put the Lord first.
ELIZABETH GEORGE

Even the most routine part of your day
can be a spiritual act of worship.
SARAH YOUNG

God wants to be in our leisure time
as much as He is in our churches and in our work.
BETH MOORE

Christ is either Lord of all, or He is not Lord at all.
HUDSON TAYLOR

Jesus Christ is the first and last, author and finisher, beginning
and end, alpha and omega, and by Him all other things hold
together. He must be first or nothing. God never comes next!
VANCE HAVNER

More from God's Word

Jesus said to him, "'You shall love the LORD your God with all your heart, with all your soul, and with all your mind.' This is the first and great commandment."
MATTHEW 22:37–38 NKJV

Be careful not to forget the LORD.
DEUTERONOMY 6:12 HCSB

We love him, because he first loved us.
1 JOHN 4:19 KJV

Do not love the world or the things that belong to the world. If anyone loves the world, love for the Father is not in him.
1 JOHN 2:15 HCSB

With my whole heart I have sought You; oh, let me not wander from Your commandments!
PSALM 119:10 NKJV

Remember This

As you establish priorities for your day and your life, God deserves first place. And you deserve the experience of putting Him there.

84

THE PROMISE: A HEALTHY FEAR OF GOD IS THE BEGINNING OF WISDOM

The fear of the LORD is the beginning of knowledge,
but fools despise wisdom and instruction.
PROVERBS 1:7 NKJV

You live in a world where too many people consider it unfashionable or unseemly to discuss the fear of God. Don't count yourself among their number. To fear God is to acknowledge His sovereignty over every aspect of His creation (including you). To fear God is to place your relationship with Him in its proper perspective (He is your master; you are His servant). To fear God is to dread the very thought of disobeying Him. And to fear God is to humble yourself in the presence of His infinite power and His infinite love.

God praises humility and punishes pride. That's why His greatest servants will always be those humble men and women who care less for their own glory and more for His glory. In God's kingdom, the only way to achieve greatness is to shun it. And the only way to be wise is to understand these facts: God is great; He is all-knowing;

and He is all-powerful. We must respect Him, and we must humbly obey His commandments, or we must accept the consequences of our misplaced pride.

When we fear the Creator—and when we honor Him by obeying His teachings—we receive God's approval and His blessings. So today, as you face the realities, and overcome the challenges, of everyday life, remember this: until you acquire a healthy, respectful fear of God's power, your education is incomplete, and so is your faith.

MORE THOUGHTS ABOUT THE FEAR OF GOD

The remarkable thing about fearing God is that when you fear God, you fear nothing else, whereas if you do not fear God, you fear everything else.
OSWALD CHAMBERS

If a person fears God, he or she has no reason to fear anything else. On the other hand, if a person does not fear God, then fear becomes a way of life.
BETH MOORE

A healthy fear of God will do much to deter us from sin.
CHARLES SWINDOLL

It is not possible that mortal men should be thoroughly conscious of the divine presence without being filled with awe.
C. H. SPURGEON

The center of God's will is our only safety.
BETSIE TEN BOOM

More from God's Word

When all has been heard, the conclusion of the matter is:
fear God and keep His commands.
ECCLESIASTES 12:13 HCSB

You shall walk after the LORD your God
and fear Him, and keep His commandments
and obey His voice; you shall serve Him and hold fast to Him.
DEUTERONOMY 13:4 NKJV

The fear of the LORD is a fountain of life.
PROVERBS 14:27 NKJV

Respect for the LORD will teach you wisdom.
If you want to be honored, you must be humble.
PROVERBS 15:33 NCV

Honour all men. Love the brotherhood.
Fear God. Honour the king.
1 PETER 2:17 KJV

A Timely Tip

Ask yourself this question: How fearful are you of disobeying God?
If the answer is "a lot," you answered correctly. But if the honest
answer is "not much," then spend a few moments thinking about
the potential consequences—perhaps the disastrous consequences—
that might result from your disobedience.

85

THE PROMISE: WHEN YOU ENCOURAGE OTHER PEOPLE, YOU'RE FULFILLING THE WILL OF CHRIST

Bear one another's burdens, and so fulfill the law of Christ.
GALATIANS 6:2 NKJV

Life is a team sport, and all of us need occasional pats on the back from our teammates. This world can be a difficult place, a place where many of our friends and family members are experiencing difficult circumstances. And since we cannot always be certain who needs our help, we should strive to speak helpful words to all who cross our paths. The Bible teaches us to choose our words carefully so as to build others up through wholesome, honest encouragement. So how can we build others up? By celebrating their victories and their accomplishments. As the old saying goes, "When someone does something good, applaud—you'll make two people happy."

Genuine encouragement should never be confused with pity. So we must guard ourselves against hosting (or joining) the pity parties that so often accompany difficult times. Instead, we must encourage each other to have faith—first in God and His only begotten Son—and then in our own abilities to use the talents God has given us for the furtherance of His kingdom and for the betterment of our own lives.

As a faithful follower of Jesus, you have every reason to be hopeful, and you have every reason to share your hopes with others. When you do, you will discover that hope, like other human emotions, is contagious. So do the world and yourself a favor: Look for the good in others and celebrate the good that you find. When you do, you'll be a powerful force of encouragement to your friends and family. And you'll be a worthy servant to your heavenly Father.

MORE THOUGHTS ABOUT ENCOURAGEMENT

Discouraged people don't need critics.
They hurt enough already. What they need is encouragement.
They need a refuge, a willing, caring, available someone.
CHARLES SWINDOLL

Developing a positive attitude means working continually
to find what is uplifting and encouraging.
BARBARA JOHNSON

I have never met a person who didn't have problems of some
kind. This is why we need one another's encouragement.
BILLY GRAHAM

Doing something positive toward another person is
a practical approach to feeling good about yourself.
BARBARA JOHNSON

MORE FROM GOD'S WORD

*But encourage each other daily, while it is still called today,
so that none of you is hardened by sin's deception.*
HEBREWS 3:13 HCSB

*Let us think about each other and help
each other to show love and do good deeds.*
HEBREWS 10:24 NCV

*So encourage each other and give
each other strength, just as you are doing now.*
1 THESSALONIANS 5:11 NCV

*When you talk, do not say harmful things,
but say what people need—words that will
help others become stronger. Then what you
say will do good to those who listen to you.*
EPHESIANS 4:29 NCV

*Now we exhort you, brethren, warn those who are unruly,
comfort the fainthearted, uphold the weak, be patient with all.*
1 THESSALONIANS 5:14 NKJV

A TIMELY TIP

Do you want to be successful? Encourage others to do the same. You can't lift other people up without lifting yourself up too. And remember the words of Oswald Chambers: "God grant that we may not hinder those who are battling their way slowly into the light."

86

THE PROMISE: JESUS WILL BEAR YOUR BURDENS

Take my yoke upon you, and learn of me; for I am meek and lowly in heart: and ye shall find rest unto your souls. For my yoke is easy, and my burden is light.

MATTHEW 11:29–30 KJV

Jesus walks with you. Are you walking with Him? Hopefully, you will choose to walk with Him today and every day of your life.

Jesus loved you so much that He endured unspeakable humiliation and suffering for you. So how will you respond to Christ's sacrifice? Will you take up your cross and follow Him (Luke 9:23), or will you choose another path? When you place your hopes squarely at the foot of the cross—when you place Jesus squarely at the center of your life—you will be blessed.

The old familiar hymn begins, "What a friend we have in Jesus." No truer words were ever penned. Jesus is the sovereign friend and ultimate savior of mankind. Christ showed enduring love for His believers by willingly sacrificing His own life so that we might have eternal life. Now, it is our turn to become His friend.

Let us love our Savior, let us praise Him, and let us share His message of hope with the world. When we do, we demonstrate that our acquaintance with the Master is not a passing fancy but is, instead, the cornerstone and the touchstone of our lives.

MORE THOUGHTS ABOUT FOLLOWING CHRIST

A disciple is a follower of Christ. That means you take on His priorities as your own. His agenda becomes your agenda. His mission becomes your mission.
CHARLES STANLEY

Be assured, if you walk with Him and look to Him, and expect help from Him, He will never fail you.
GEORGE MUELLER

The crucial question for each of us is this: What do you think of Jesus, and do you yet have a personal acquaintance with Him?
HANNAH WHITALL SMITH

Choose Jesus Christ! Deny yourself, take up the Cross, and follow Him, for the world must be shown. The world must see, in us, a discernible, visible, startling difference.
ELISABETH ELLIOT

Christ is not valued at all unless He is valued above all.
ST. AUGUSTINE

More from God's Word

Then He said to them all, "If anyone wants to come with Me, he must deny himself, take up his cross daily, and follow Me."
LUKE 9:23 HCSB

But whoever keeps His word, truly in him the love of God is perfected. This is how we know we are in Him: the one who says he remains in Him should walk just as He walked.
1 JOHN 2:5–6 HCSB

Walk in a manner worthy of the God who calls you into His own kingdom and glory.
1 THESSALONIANS 2:12 NASB

For we walk by faith, not by sight.
2 CORINTHIANS 5:7 HCSB

Whoever is not willing to carry the cross and follow me is not worthy of me. Those who try to hold on to their lives will give up true life. Those who give up their lives for me will hold on to true life.
MATTHEW 10:38–39 NCV

Remember This

Following Christ is a matter of obedience. If you want to be a little more like Jesus, learn about His teachings, follow in His footsteps, and obey His commandments.

87

THE PROMISE: GOD PROVIDES WISDOM

But if any of you lacks wisdom, let him ask of God, who gives to all generously and without reproach, and it will be given to him.

JAMES 1:5 NASB

All the wisdom that you'll ever need to live a meaningful life can be found in a single book: the Bible. God's Word guides us along a path that leads to abundance and eternal life. When we embrace Biblical teachings and follow God's Son, we're protected. But when we wander from His path, we inevitably suffer the consequences of our mistaken priorities.

In theory, all of us would prefer to be wise, but not all of us are willing to make the sacrifices that are required to gain real wisdom. To become wise, we must do more than spout platitudes, recite verses, or repeat aphorisms. We must not only speak wisely; we must live wisely. We must not only learn the lessons of the Christian life; we must live by them.

Today, as you think about the best way to live and rise above difficult circumstances, remember that God's wisdom and God's promises can be found in a book that's already on your bookshelf: His book. Read, heed, and live accordingly.

More Thoughts about Wisdom

Wisdom is the right use of knowledge.
To know is not to be wise. There is no fool
so great as the knowing fool. But, to know
how to use knowledge is to have wisdom.
C. H. Spurgeon

True wisdom is marked by willingness
to listen and a sense of knowing when to yield.
Elizabeth George

Wisdom is the power to see
and the inclination to choose the best
and highest goal, together with the
surest means of attaining it.
J. I. Packer

Wisdom is doing now what you
are going to be happy with later on.
Joyce Meyer

Knowledge can be found in books or in school.
Wisdom, on the other hand,
starts with God . . . and ends there.
Marie T. Freeman

More from God's Word

The fear of the LORD is the beginning of knowledge,
but fools despise wisdom and instruction.
PROVERBS 1:7 NKJV

Get wisdom—how much better it is than gold!
And get understanding—it is preferable to silver.
PROVERBS 16:16 HCSB

But the wisdom that is from above is first pure,
then peaceable, gentle, willing to yield, full of mercy
and good fruits, without partiality and without hypocrisy.
JAMES 3:17 NKJV

He that walketh with wise men shall be wise:
but a companion of fools shall be destroyed.
PROVERBS 13:20 KJV

Who among you is wise and understanding? Let him show
by his good behavior his deeds in the gentleness of wisdom.
JAMES 3:13 NASB

A Timely Tip

Need wisdom? God's got it. If you want it, then study God's Word
and associate with godly people.

88

THE PROMISE: JESUS OFFERS A BRAND OF CONTENTMENT THAT THE WORLD CANNOT PROVIDE

*Come unto me, all ye that labour
and are heavy laden, and I will give you rest.*
MATTHEW 11:28 KJV

When we conduct ourselves in ways that are opposed to God's commandments, we rob ourselves of God's peace. When we fall prey to the temptations and distractions of our irreverent age, we rob ourselves of God's blessings. When we become preoccupied with material possessions or personal status, we forfeit the contentment that is rightfully ours in Christ.

So where can we find genuine contentment? Is it a result of wealth, or power, or fame? Hardly. Genuine contentment is a gift from God to those who follow His commandments and accept His Son. When Christ dwells at the center of our families and our lives, contentment will belong to us just as surely as we belong to Him.

Are you a contented Christian? If so, then you're well aware of the healing power of the risen Christ. But if your spirit is temporarily troubled, perhaps you need to focus less upon your own priorities and more upon God's priorities. When you do, you'll rediscover this life-changing truth: Genuine contentment begins with God . . . and ends there.

More Thoughts about Contentment

Contentment is possible when we stop striving for more.
CHARLES SWINDOLL

Those who are God's without reserve are,
in every sense, content.
HANNAH WHITALL SMITH

No matter what you're facing, embrace life in trust
and contentment based on your faith in Jesus.
ELIZABETH GEORGE

When you truly know God, you have energy to serve Him,
boldness to share Him, and contentment in Him.
J. I. PACKER

The happiness which brings enduring worth to life
is not the superficial happiness that is dependent
on circumstances. It is the happiness and contentment that fills
the soul in the midst of the most distressing of circumstances.
BILLY GRAHAM

MORE FROM GOD'S WORD

I have learned in whatever state I am, to be content.
PHILIPPIANS 4:11 NKJV

But godliness with contentment is a great gain.
1 TIMOTHY 6:6 HCSB

*Make sure that your character is free from
the love of money, being content with what you have;
for He Himself has said, "I will never desert you,
nor will I ever forsake you."*
HEBREWS 13:5 NASB

*A tranquil heart is life to the body,
but jealousy is rottenness to the bones.*
PROVERBS 14:30 HCSB

*The peace of God, which passeth all understanding,
shall keep your hearts and minds through Christ Jesus.*
PHILIPPIANS 4:7 KJV

A TIMELY TIP

Be contented where you are, even if it's not exactly where you want to end up. God has something wonderful in store for you—and remember that God's timing is perfect—so be patient, trust God, do your best, and expect the best.

89

THE PROMISE: THE LORD WILL GUIDE YOU IF YOU LET HIM

Trust in the LORD with all your heart, and lean not on your own understanding; in all your ways acknowledge Him, and He shall direct your paths.

PROVERBS 3:5–6 NKJV

When we ask for God's guidance, with our hearts and minds open to His direction, He will lead us along a path of His choosing. But for many of us, listening to God is hard. We have so many things we want, and so many needs to pray for, that we spend far more time talking at God than we do listening to Him.

Corrie ten Boom observed, "God's guidance is even more important than common sense. I can declare that the deepest darkness is outshone by the light of Jesus." These words remind us that life is best lived when we seek the Lord's direction early and often.

Our Father has many ways to make Himself known. Our challenge is to make ourselves open to His instruction. So if you're unsure of your next step, trust God's promises and talk to Him often. When you do, He'll guide your steps today, tomorrow, and forever.

More Thoughts about God's Guidance

*God never leads us to do anything
that is contrary to the Bible.*
BILLY GRAHAM

*When we are obedient,
God guides our steps and our stops.*
CORRIE TEN BOOM

*Are you serious about wanting God's guidance
to become a personal reality in your life?
The first step is to tell God that you know you
can't manage your own life; that you need His help.*
CATHERINE MARSHALL

*The will of God will never take us where
the grace of God cannot sustain us.*
BILLY GRAHAM

*As you walk through the valley of the unknown,
you will find the footprints of Jesus
both in front of you and beside you.*
CHARLES STANLEY

MORE FROM GOD'S WORD

Yet LORD, You are our Father; we are the clay,
and You are our potter; we all are the work of Your hands.
ISAIAH 64:8 HCSB

The LORD says, "I will guide you along the best pathway
for your life. I will advise you and watch over you."
PSALM 32:8 NLT

Teach me to do Your will, for You are my God;
Your Spirit is good. Lead me in the land of uprightness.
PSALM 143:10 NKJV

Shew me thy ways, O LORD; teach me thy paths.
Lead me in thy truth, and teach me: for thou art
the God of my salvation; on thee do I wait all the day.
PSALM 25:4–5 KJV

Morning by morning he wakens me and opens my
understanding to his will. The Sovereign LORD
has spoken to me, and I have listened.
ISAIAH 50:4–5 NLT

A TIMELY TIP

Would you like God's guidance? Then ask Him for it. When you pray for guidance, God will give it, so ask.

90

THE PROMISE: GOD HEARS YOUR PRAYERS

But God has listened; he has heard my prayer.
PSALM 66:19 NCV

God has promised to hear your prayers. So here are a few questions worth considering: Is prayer an integral part of your daily life or is it a hit-or-miss habit? Do you "pray without ceasing," or is your prayer life an afterthought? Do you regularly pray in the quiet moments of the early morning, or do you bow your head only when others are watching?

As Christians, we are instructed to pray often. But it is important to note that genuine prayer requires much more than bending our knees and closing our eyes. Heartfelt prayer is an attitude of the heart.

If your prayers have become more a matter of habit than a matter of passion, you're robbing yourself of a deeper relationship with the Lord. So how can you rectify this situation? By praying more frequently and more fervently. When you do, God will shower you with His blessings, His grace, and His love.

More Thoughts about Prayer

Prayer is our lifeline to God.
BILLY GRAHAM

*Two wings are necessary to lift
our souls toward God:
prayer and praise. Prayer asks.
Praise accepts the answer.*
LETTIE COWMAN

*Don't pray when you feel like it.
Have an appointment with the Lord and keep it.*
CORRIE TEN BOOM

*It is impossible to overstate
the need for prayer in the fabric of family life.*
JAMES DOBSON

*Any concern that is too small
to be turned into a prayer is too small
to be made into a burden.*
CORRIE TEN BOOM

MORE FROM GOD'S WORD

Is anyone among you suffering? He should pray.
JAMES 5:13 HCSB

Confess your trespasses to one another, and pray for one another, that you may be healed. The effective, fervent prayer of a righteous man avails much.
JAMES 5:16 NKJV

And whenever you stand praying, if you have anything against anyone, forgive him, so that your Father in heaven will also forgive you your wrongdoing.
MARK 11:25 HCSB

Ask, and it will be given to you; seek, and you will find; knock, and it will be opened to you. For everyone who asks receives, and he who seeks finds, and to him who knocks it will be opened.
MATTHEW 7:7–8 NASB

Rejoice always, pray without ceasing, in everything give thanks; for this is the will of God in Christ Jesus for you.
1 THESSALONIANS 5:16–18 NKJV

REMEMBER THIS

God does not answer all of our prayers in the affirmative. When we are disappointed by the realities of life here on earth, we should remember that our prayers are always answered by an all-knowing God, and that we must trust Him, whatever the answer.

91

THE PROMISE:
JESUS IS THE LIGHT THAT
CASTS OUT DARKNESS

I have come as a light into the world, so that everyone
who believes in Me would not remain in darkness.

JOHN 12:46 HCSB

Jesus is the light of the world. And God wants us to live in the light of His truth, not in the darkness of deception and despair. The Lord wants us to live abundantly, in accordance with His teachings. And He wants us to be a worthy example to our families, to our friends, and to the world.

Every day, we make decisions that can bring us closer to God, or not. When we follow closely in the footsteps of Christ, we experience His blessings and His peace. But when we stray far from God's path, we forfeit many of the gifts that He has in store for us.

You live in a dangerous, distraction-filled world, brimming with temptations. Your task, of course, to live in the light and avoid the darkness. When you do, you'll serve as a powerful example and a positive role model in a world that surely needs both.

More Thoughts about Walking in the Light

*God's Word is a light not only
to our path but also to our thinking.
Place it in your heart today,
and you will never walk in darkness.*

Joni Eareckson Tada

*May not a single moment of my life
be spent outside the light,
love, and joy of God's presence.*

Andrew Murray

*Virtue, even attempted virtue, brings light;
indulgence brings fog.*

C. S. Lewis

*Fold the arms of your faith and wait
in quietness until the light
goes up in your darkness.*

George MacDonald

*It is not darkness you are going to,
for God is Light. It is not lonely,
for Christ is with you.
It is not unknown country, for Christ is there.*

Charles Kingsley

More from God's Word

For you were once darkness, but now you are light
in the Lord. Walk as children of light—for the fruit
of the light results in all goodness, righteousness,
and truth—discerning what is pleasing to the Lord.
EPHESIANS 5:8–10 HCSB

LORD, You are my lamp; the LORD illuminates my darkness.
2 SAMUEL 22:29 HCSB

He who loves his brother abides in the light,
and there is no cause for stumbling in him.
1 JOHN 2:10 NKJV

You are the light that gives light to the world. . . .
In the same way, you should be a light for other people.
Live so that they will see the good things you
do and will praise your Father in heaven.
MATTHEW 5:14, 16 NCV

This is the message which we have heard from Him and declare
to you, that God is light and in Him is no darkness at all.
1 JOHN 1:5 NKJV

A Timely Tip

Jesus is the light of the world. Make sure that you are capturing and reflecting His light.

92

THE PROMISE:
IF YOU SEEK GOD'S
GUIDANCE, HE WILL
OFFER IT DAY BY DAY

Morning by morning he wakens me
and opens my understanding to his will.
The Sovereign LORD has spoken to me, and I have listened.
ISAIAH 50:4–5 NLT

Every new day is a gift from the Creator, a gift that allows each of us to say thank You by spending time with the Giver. When we begin the day with our Bibles open and our hearts attuned to God, we are inevitably blessed by the promises we find in His Word.

During the quiet moments we spend with the Lord, He guides us; He leads us; He touches our hearts. And when we are experiencing trials or hardships, the time we spend with the Creator provides us with two things we desperately need: perspective and hope.

Each day of your life has 1,440 minutes, and God deserves a few of them. And you deserve the experience of spending a few quiet minutes every morning with your Creator. So if you haven't already done so, establish the habit of spending time with the Lord every day of the week. It's a habit that will change your day and revolutionize your life. When you give the Lord your undivided attention, everything changes, including you.

MORE THOUGHTS ABOUT YOUR DAILY DEVOTIONAL

Make it the first morning business of your life to understand some part of the Bible clearly, and make it your daily business to obey it.
JOHN RUSKIN

Relying on God has to begin all over again every day as if nothing had yet been done.
C. S. LEWIS

Begin each day with God. It will change your priorities.
ELIZABETH GEORGE

Doesn't God deserve the best minutes of your day?
BILLY GRAHAM

Whatever is your best time in the day, give that to communion with God.
HUDSON TAYLOR

More from God's Word

It is good to give thanks to the Lord,
and to sing praises to Your name, O Most High.
Psalm 92:1 NKJV

Heaven and earth will pass away,
but My words will never pass away.
Matthew 24:35 HCSB

Thy word is a lamp unto my feet, and a light unto my path.
Psalm 119:105 KJV

Early the next morning, while it was still dark,
Jesus woke and left the house.
He went to a lonely place, where he prayed.
Mark 1:35 NCV

But grow in the grace and knowledge
of our Lord and Savior Jesus Christ.
To Him be the glory both now and to the day of eternity.
2 Peter 3:18 HCSB

A Timely Tip

Would you like a foolproof formula for a better life? Here it is: Stay in close contact with God. Hannah Whitall Smith wrote, "The crucial question for each of us is this: What do you think of Jesus, and do you yet have a personal acquaintance with Him?" Think about your relationship with Jesus—what it is and what it could be.

93

THE PROMISE: OBEDIENCE TO THE LORD RESULTS IN PEACEFUL CONFIDENCE

The result of righteousness will be peace; the effect of righteousness will be quiet confidence forever.

ISAIAH 32:17 HCSB

Would you like a time-tested formula for surviving tough times and rising above difficult circumstances? Here is a formula that is proven and true: Seek God's approval in every aspect of your life. Does this sound too simple? Perhaps it is simple, but it is also the only way to reap the greatest rewards that God has in store for you.

So today, take every step of your journey with God as your traveling companion. Read His Word, trust His promises, and follow His commandments. Support only those activities that further God's kingdom and your own spiritual growth. Be an example of righteous living to your friends, to your neighbors, to your coworkers, and to your family. Then reap the blessings that God has promised to all those who live according to His will and His Word.

More Thoughts
about Righteousness

We have two natures within us,
both struggling for mastery. Which one will dominate us?
It depends on which one we feed.
Billy Graham

Virtue, even attempted virtue, brings light;
indulgence brings fog.
C. S. Lewis

Let us never suppose that obedience is impossible
or that holiness is meant only for a select few.
Our Shepherd leads us in paths of righteousness—
not for our name's sake but for His.
Elisabeth Elliot

Never support an experience which does not have God as its
source and faith in God as its result.
Oswald Chambers

You can only learn what obedience is by obeying.
Dietrich Bonhoeffer

More from God's Word

Discipline yourself for the purpose of godliness.
1 Timothy 4:7 NASB

And let us not grow weary while doing good,
for in due season we shall reap if we do not lose heart.
Galatians 6:9 NKJV

But godliness with contentment is a great gain.
1 Timothy 6:6 HCSB

Now by this we know that we know Him,
if we keep His commandments.
1 John 2:3 NKJV

For the eyes of the LORD are over the righteous,
and his ears are open unto their prayers:
but the face of the LORD is against them that do evil.
1 Peter 3:12 KJV

A Timely Tip

Today, consider the value of living a life that is pleasing to God. And while you're at it, think about the rewards that are likely to be yours when you do the right thing day in and day out.

94

THE PROMISE: GOD HAS A PLAN FOR YOU

But as it is written: What eye did not see and ear
did not hear, and what never entered the human mind—
God prepared this for those who love Him.

1 CORINTHIANS 2:9 HCSB

Why did God put me here?" It's a simple question to ask and, at times, a very complicated question to answer.

As you seek to discover (or, perhaps, to rediscover) God's plan for your life, you should start by remembering this: you are here because God put you here, and He did so for a very good reason: His reason.

At times, you may be confident that you are doing God's will. But on other occasions, you may be uncertain about the direction that your life should take. At times, you may wander aimlessly in a wilderness of your own making. And sometimes, you may even struggle mightily against God in a vain effort to find success and happiness through your own means, not His. But wherever you find yourself—whether on the mountaintops, in the valleys, or at the crossroads of life—you can be sure that God is there, and you can be assured that He has a plan.

Once you manage to align yourself with God's plan for your life, you will be energized, you will be enthused, and you will be blessed. That's why you should strive to understand what it is that God wants you to do. But how can you know precisely what God's intentions are? The answer, of course, is that even the most well-intentioned believers face periods of uncertainty and doubt about the direction of their lives. So, too, will you.

When you arrive at one of life's inevitable crossroads, that's the moment when you should turn your thoughts, and lift your prayers, to the Lord. When you do, He will make Himself known to you in a time and manner of His choosing. When you discover His plan for your life, you will experience abundance, peace, joy, and power—God's power. And that's the only kind of power that really matters.

MORE THOUGHTS ABOUT GOD'S PLAN

One of the wonderful things about being a Christian is the knowledge that God has a plan for our lives.
WARREN WIERSBE

God has no problems, only plans.
There is never panic in heaven.
CORRIE TEN BOOM

Do not let Satan deceive you into being afraid of God's plans for your life.
R. A. TORREY

God will not permit any troubles to come upon us unless He has a specific plan by which great blessing can come out of the difficulty.
PETER MARSHALL

More from God's Word

*For My thoughts are not your thoughts, and your ways are not
My ways. . . . For as heaven is higher than earth, so My ways
are higher than your ways, and My thoughts than your thoughts.*

ISAIAH 55:8–9 HCSB

*And yet, O LORD, you are our Father.
We are the clay, and you are the potter.
We are all formed by your hand.*

ISAIAH 64:8 NLT

*For whoever does the will of God
is My brother and My sister and mother.*

MARK 3:35 NKJV

*It is God who is at work in you, both to will
and to work for His good pleasure.*

PHILIPPIANS 2:13 NASB

*We must do the works of Him who sent Me while it is day.
Night is coming when no one can work.*

JOHN 9:4 HCSB

A Timely Tip

God has a wonderful plan for your life. And the time to start looking
for that plan—and living it—is now. Discovering God's plan begins
with prayer, but it doesn't end there. You've also got to work at it.

95

THE PROMISE:
GOD IS AT WORK
IN YOUR LIFE

*For it is God who is working in you, enabling you both
to desire and to work out His good purpose.*
PHILIPPIANS 2:13 HCSB

God does not do things by accident; He has a plan for our world
and our lives. He is willful and intentional. We can never fully comprehend the will of God, but as believers in a benevolent heavenly
Father, we must always trust the will of God.

Before His crucifixion, Jesus went to the Mount of Olives and
poured out His heart to God (Luke 22). Jesus knew of the agony
that He was destined to endure, but He also knew that God's will
must be done. We, like our Savior, face trials that bring fear and
trembling to the very depths of our souls, but like Christ, we, too,
must ultimately seek God's will, not our own.

As this day unfolds, seek God's will and obey His Word. When
you entrust your life to Him completely and without reservation, He
will give you the strength to meet any challenge, the courage to face
any trial, and the wisdom to live in His righteousness and in His peace.

MORE THOUGHTS ABOUT GOD'S WILL

Each and every decision you make,
regardless of its level of intensity,
is vitally important as you seek to do God's will.
ELIZABETH GEORGE

The center of God's will is our only safety.
BETSIE TEN BOOM

It is possible to see God's will
in every circumstance and to accept
it with singing instead of complaining.
LETTIE COWMAN

Life's trials are not easy.
But in God's will, each has a purpose.
Often He uses them to enlarge you.
WARREN WIERSBE

To know the will of God
is the highest of all wisdom.
BILLY GRAHAM

More from God's Word

Teach me to do Your will, for You are my God;
Your Spirit is good.
Lead me in the land of uprightness.
PSALM 143:10 NKJV

Commit to the LORD whatever you do,
and he will establish your plans.
PROVERBS 16:3 NIV

Then Jesus explained: "My nourishment
comes from doing the will of God,
who sent me, and from finishing his work."
JOHN 4:34 NLT

For it is better, if it is the will of God,
to suffer for doing good than for doing evil.
1 PETER 3:17 NKJV

He is the LORD. He will do what He thinks is good.
1 SAMUEL 3:18 HCSB

Remember This

Even when you cannot understand God's plans, you must trust them. If you place yourself in the center of God's will, He will provide for your needs and direct your path.

96

THE PROMISE: BECAUSE YOUR ULTIMATE REWARD IS IN HEAVEN, YOU HAVE EVERY REASON TO REJOICE

Be glad and rejoice, because your reward is great in heaven.
MATTHEW 5:12 HCSB

Attitudes are the mental filters through which we view and interpret the world around us. People with positive attitudes look for the best and usually find it. People burdened by chronically negative attitudes are not so fortunate.

God created you in His own image, and He wants you to experience joy, contentment, peace, and abundance. But God will not force you to experience these things; you must claim them for yourself. Your attitude will inevitably determine the quality and direction of your day and your life. That's why it's so important to stay positive.

The Christian life can, and should, be cause for celebration. After all, every new day is a gift, every new circumstance an opportunity to praise and to serve. So how will you direct your thoughts today?

Will you focus on God's love? Will you hold fast to His promises and trust His plan for your life? Or will you allow your thoughts to be hijacked by negativity, fear, and doubt? If you're a thoughtful believer, you'll think optimistically about yourself and your future. And while you're at it, you'll give thanks to the Creator for more blessings than you can count.

More Thoughts about Maintaining a Positive Attitude

Come up from the lowlands; there are heights yet to climb.
You cannot do healthful thinking in the lowlands.
Look to the mountaintop for faith.
MARY McLEOD BETHUNE

Attitude is the mind's paintbrush; it can color any situation.
BARBARA JOHNSON

Keep your feet on the ground, but let your heart soar
as high as it will. Refuse to be average or to surrender
to the chill of your spiritual environment.
A. W. TOZER

A positive attitude will have positive results
because attitudes are contagious.
ZIG ZIGLAR

Outlook determines outcome and attitude determines action.
WARREN WIERSBE

MORE FROM GOD'S WORD

Finally, brothers, rejoice. Become mature,
be encouraged, be of the same mind,
be at peace, and the God of love
and peace will be with you.
2 CORINTHIANS 13:11 HCSB

A merry heart makes a cheerful countenance.
PROVERBS 15:13 NKJV

You must have the same attitude that Christ Jesus had.
PHILIPPIANS 2:5 NLT

Rejoice always; pray without ceasing.
1 THESSALONIANS 5:16–17 NASB

This is the day the LORD has made;
let us rejoice and be glad in it.
PSALM 118:24 HCSB

A TIMELY TIP

Today, create a positive attitude by focusing on opportunities, not roadblocks. Of course you may have experienced disappointments in the past, and you will undoubtedly experience some setbacks in the future. But don't invest large amounts of energy focusing on past misfortunes. Instead, look to the future with optimism and hope.

97

THE PROMISE: GOD WILL BLESS YOU IN YOUR SPIRITUAL GROWTH

I remind you to fan into flames the spiritual gift God gave you.
2 TIMOTHY 1:6 NLT

When it comes to your faith, God doesn't intend for you to stand still. He wants you to keep moving and growing. In fact, God's plan for you includes a lifetime of prayer, praise, and spiritual growth.

Many of life's most important lessons are painful to learn. During times of heartbreak and hardship, we must be courageous and we must be patient, knowing that in His own time, God will heal us if we invite Him into our hearts.

Spiritual growth need not take place only in times of adversity. We must seek to grow in our knowledge and love of the Lord every day that we live. In those quiet moments when we open our hearts to the Lord, the One who made us keeps remaking us. He gives us direction, perspective, wisdom, and courage.

Are you as mature as you're ever going to be? Hopefully not. When it comes to your faith, God doesn't intend for you to become "fully grown," at least not in this lifetime. In fact, the Lord still has important lessons that He intends to teach you. So ask yourself this: What lesson is God trying to teach me today? And then go about the business of learning it.

More Thoughts about Spiritual Growth

Daily Bible reading is essential to victorious living and real Christian growth.
BILLY GRAHAM

The Scriptures were not given for our information, but for our transformation.
D. L. MOODY

The vigor of our spiritual lives will be in exact proportion to the place held by the Bible in our lives and in our thoughts.
GEORGE MUELLER

Grow, dear friends, but grow, I beseech you, in God's way, which is the only true way.
HANNAH WHITALL SMITH

Kindness in this world will do much to help others, not only to come into the light, but also to grow in grace day by day.
FANNY CROSBY

More from God's Word

But endurance must do its complete work, so that
you may be mature and complete, lacking nothing.
JAMES 1:4 HCSB

But grow in the grace and knowledge of our Lord and Savior
Jesus Christ. To Him be the glory both now and forever. Amen.
2 PETER 3:18 NKJV

And be not conformed to this world: but be ye transformed
by the renewing of your mind, that ye may prove what
is that good, and acceptable, and perfect will of God.
ROMANS 12:2 KJV

Leave inexperience behind, and you will live;
pursue the way of understanding.
PROVERBS 9:6 HCSB

So let us stop going over the basic teachings
about Christ again and again. Let us go on instead
and become mature in our understanding.
HEBREWS 6:1 NLT

A Timely Tip

Times of change can be times of growth. Elisabeth Elliot reminds us that tough times can lead to a renewal of spirit: "If the leaves had not been let go to fall and wither, if the tree had not consented to be a skeleton for many months, there would be no new life rising, no bud, no flower, no fruit, no seed, no new generation." So remember: spiritual maturity is always a journey, never a destination.

98

THE PROMISE: YOUR TESTIMONY MATTERS

For God has not given us a spirit of fear and timidity,
but of power, love, and self-discipline.
So never be ashamed to tell others about our Lord.

2 TIMOTHY 1:7–8 NLT

Have you made the decision to allow Christ to reign over your heart? If so, you have an important story to tell: yours.

Your personal testimony is profoundly important, but perhaps because of shyness (or because of the fear of being rebuffed), you've been hesitant to share your experiences. If so, you should start paying less attention to your own insecurities and more attention to the message that God wants you to share with the world.

When we let other people know the details of our faith, we assume an important responsibility—the responsibility of making certain that our words are reinforced by our actions. When we share our testimonies, we must also be willing to serve as examples of obedience and maturity.

Do you sincerely want to follow in the footsteps of God's only begotten Son? If so, you must also be willing to talk about Him. The time to express your belief in Him is now. You know how He has touched your own heart; help Him do the same for others.

MORE THOUGHTS ABOUT YOUR TESTIMONY

What is your story? Be ready to share it
when the Lord gives you the opportunity.
BILLY GRAHAM

Heads are won by reasoning,
but hearts are won by witness-bearing.
C. H. SPURGEON

When your heart is ablaze with the love of God,
then you love other people—especially the
rip-snorting sinners—so much that you dare to tell
them about Jesus with no apologies and no fear.
CATHERINE MARSHALL

The enemy's hope for Christians is that we will
either be so ineffective we have no testimony,
or we'll ruin the one we have.
BETH MOORE

How many people have you made homesick for God?
OSWALD CHAMBERS

MORE FROM GOD'S WORD

And I say to you, anyone who acknowledges Me before men, the Son of Man will also acknowledge him before the angels of God.
LUKE 12:8 HCSB

You must worship Christ as Lord of your life. And if someone asks about your hope as a believer, always be ready to explain it.
1 PETER 3:15 NLT

All those who stand before others and say they believe in me, I will say before my Father in heaven that they belong to me.
MATTHEW 10:32 NCV

When they had prayed, the place where they were assembled was shaken, and they were all filled with the Holy Spirit and began to speak God's message with boldness.
ACTS 4:31 HCSB

Then He said to them, "Go into all the world and preach the gospel to the whole creation."
MARK 16:15 HCSB

A TIMELY TIP

What should you do if you're uncomfortable talking about your faith? You should remember this: you're not giving the State of the Union Address—You're having a conversation. And besides, if you're not sure what to say, a good place to start is by asking questions, not making speeches.

99

THE PROMISE: WHEN YOU ASK, HE RESPONDS

Ask, and it will be given to you; seek,
and you will find; knock, and it will be opened to you.
For everyone who asks receives, and he who seeks finds,
and to him who knocks it will be opened.

MATTHEW 7:7–8 NASB

The Lord invites us to ask Him for the things we need, and He promises to hear our prayers as well as our thoughts. The Lord is always available, and He's always ready to help us. And He knows precisely what we need. But He still instructs us to ask.

Do you make a habit of asking God for the things you need? Hopefully so. After all, the Father most certainly has a plan for your life. And He can do great things through you if you have the courage to ask for His guidance and His help. So be fervent in prayer and don't hesitate to ask the Creator for the tools you need to accomplish His plan for your life. Then get busy and expect the best. When you do your part, God will most certainly do His part. And great things are bound to happen.

The Lord always hears your prayers, and He always responds in His own way and in His own time. Your task, of course, is to make God a full partner in every aspect of your life *and* to seek His guidance prayerfully, confidently, and often.

MORE THOUGHTS ABOUT ASKING GOD FOR THE THINGS YOU NEED

We honor God by asking for great things when they are a part of His promise. We dishonor Him and cheat ourselves when we ask for molehills where He has promised mountains.
VANCE HAVNER

We get into trouble when we think we know what to do and we stop asking God if we're doing it.
STORMIE OMARTIAN

By asking in Jesus' name, we're making a request not only in His authority, but also for His interests and His benefit.
SHIRLEY DOBSON

Often I have made a request of God with earnest pleadings even backed up with Scripture, only to have Him say "No" because He had something better in store.
RUTH BELL GRAHAM

God will help us become the people we are meant to be, if only we will ask Him.
HANNAH WHITALL SMITH

MORE FROM GOD'S WORD

Until now you have asked for nothing in My name.
Ask and you will receive,
that your joy may be complete.

Do not be anxious about anything,
but in every sitiuation, by prayer and petition,
with thanksgiving, present your requests to God.

PHILIPPIANS 4:6 NIV

The effective prayer of a righteous
man can accomplish much.

JAMES 5:16 NASB

Your Father knows the things you
have need of before you ask Him.

MATTHEW 6:8 NKJV

You did not choose me, but I chose you and appointed you so
that you might go and bear fruit—fruit that will last—and so
that whatever you ask in my name the Father will give you.

JOHN 15:16 NIV

A TIMELY TIP

Today, think of a specific need that is weighing heavily on your heart. Then, spend a few quiet moments asking God for His guidance and for His help.

100

THE PROMISE:
YOU CAN HAVE
ETERNAL LIFE

*For God so loved the world, that he gave
his only begotten Son, that whosoever believeth
in him should not perish, but have everlasting life.*

JOHN 3:16 KJV

The Bible makes this promise: When you believe in Jesus and give your heart to Him, you will receive an incredible gift—the gift of eternal life. This promise is unambiguous, and it's the cornerstone of the Christian faith.

Jesus is not only the light of the world; He is also its salvation. He came to this earth so that we should not perish but, instead, should spend eternity with Him. What a glorious gift; what a priceless opportunity.

As mere mortals, we cannot fully understand the scope, and thus the value, of eternal life. Our vision is limited but God's is not. He sees all things; He knows all things; and His plans for you extend throughout eternity.

If you haven't already done so, this moment is the perfect moment to turn your life over to God's only begotten Son. When you give your heart to the Son, you belong to the Father today, tomorrow, and for all eternity.

MORE THOUGHTS
ABOUT ACCEPTING CHRIST

Trust God's Word and His power more than
you trust your own feelings and experiences.
Remember, your Rock is Christ, and it is the sea
that ebbs and flows with the tides, not Him.
LETTIE COWMAN

Blessed assurance, Jesus is mine!
O what a foretaste of glory divine!
FANNY CROSBY

Ultimately, our relationship with Christ
is the one thing we cannot do without.
BETH MOORE

The crucial question for each of us is this:
What do you think of Jesus, and do you yet
have a personal acquaintance with Him?
HANNAH WHITALL SMITH

The destiny of your own soul is in
your own hands by the choice you make.
BILLY GRAHAM

MORE FROM GOD'S WORD

*And this is the testimony: God has given us eternal life,
and this life is in His Son. The one who has the Son has life.
The one who doesn't have the Son of God does not have life.*
1 JOHN 5:11–12 HCSB

*For the wages of sin is death, but the gift
of God is eternal life in Christ Jesus our Lord.*
ROMANS 6:23 NIV

*The Spirit of God, who raised Jesus from the dead,
lives in you. And just as he raised Christ
from the dead, he will give life to your
mortal bodies by this same Spirit living within you.*
ROMANS 8:11 NLT

*Therefore we were buried with Him by baptism into death,
in order that, just as Christ was raised from the dead by the
glory of the Father, so we too may walk in a new way of life.*
ROMANS 6:4 HCSB

*I am the good shepherd. The good shepherd
lays down his life for the sheep.*
JOHN 10:11 NIV

REMEMBER THIS

God offers you the priceless gift of eternal life. If you have not yet
accepted His gift, the appropriate moment to do so is now.

More Promises
from God's Word

PUT THE LORD IN HIS
RIGHTFUL PLACE: FIRST PLACE

Therefore, whether you eat or drink,
or whatever you do, do all to the glory of God.
1 CORINTHIANS 10:31 NKJV

For this is the love of God,
that we keep His commandments.
And His commandments are not burdensome.
1 JOHN 5:3 NKJV

How happy is everyone who fears the LORD,
who walks in His ways!
PSALM 128:1 HCSB

But prove yourselves doers of the word,
and not merely hearers who delude themselves.
JAMES 1:22 NASB

We love him, because he first loved us.
1 JOHN 4:19 KJV

Trust God's Promises

Sustain me as You promised, and I will live;
do not let me be ashamed of my hope.
PSALM 119:116 HCSB

As for God, his way is perfect:
the word of the LORD is tried:
he is a buckler to all those that trust in him.
PSALM 18:30 KJV

They will bind themselves to the LORD
with an eternal covenant
that will never again be forgotten.
JEREMIAH 50:5 NLT

My God is my rock, in whom I take refuge,
my shield and the horn of my salvation.
2 SAMUEL 22:3 NIV

He heeded their prayer, because they put their trust in him.
1 CHRONICLES 5:20 NKJV

HAVE THE COURAGE TO TRUST GOD

Trust in the LORD with all your heart,
and lean not on your own understanding;
in all your ways acknowledge Him,
and He shall direct your paths.
PROVERBS 3:5–6 NKJV

In quietness and trust is your strength.
ISAIAH 30:15 NASB

The LORD is my rock, my fortress,
and my deliverer, my God, my mountain
where I seek refuge. My shield,
the horn of my salvation, my stronghold,
my refuge, and my Savior.
2 SAMUEL 22:2–3 HCSB

Those who trust in the LORD are like Mount Zion.
It cannot be shaken; it remains forever.
PSALM 125:1 HCSB

TRUST THE LORD
WHEN TIMES ARE TOUGH

*We are hard-pressed on every side, yet not crushed;
we are perplexed, but not in despair.*
2 CORINTHIANS 4:8 NKJV

*I called to the LORD in my distress;
I called to my God. From His temple He heard my voice.*
2 SAMUEL 22:7 HCSB

*God blesses those who patiently endure testing
and temptation. Afterward they will receive
the crown of life that God has
promised to those who love him.*
JAMES 1:12 NLT

*He heals the brokenhearted
and binds up their wounds.*
PSALM 147:3 HCSB

GOD HAS A PLAN FOR YOU

Trust in the LORD with all your heart,
and lean not on your own understanding;
in all your ways acknowledge Him,
and He shall direct your paths.
PROVERBS 3:5–6 NKJV

The LORD sees every heart and understands
and knows every plan and thought.
If you seek him, you will find him.
1 CHRONICLES 28:9 NLT

Yet LORD, You are our Father;
we are the clay, and You are our potter;
we all are the work of Your hands.
ISAIAH 64:8 HCSB

It is God who is at work in you,
both to will and to work for His good pleasure.
PHILIPPIANS 2:13 NASB

We must do the works of Him
who sent Me while it is day.
Night is coming when no one can work.
JOHN 9:4 HCSB